STOLEN FROM MY BOSOM

STOLEN FROM MY BOSOM

Krystal Love

JANUS PUBLISHING COMPANY
London England

First Published in Great Britain 2005
by Janus Publishing Company Ltd,
105-107 Gloucester Place,
London W1U 6BY

www.januspublishing.co.uk

British Library Cataloguing-in-Publication Data
A catalogue record for this book
is available from the British Library

ISBN 1 85756 564 9

Cover Design Nathan Cording
Printed and bound in Great Britain

Previous Work by the Author

The Tarot Companion

House Rules

Blind to the Molesting Hands

I would like to dedicate *Stolen From My Bosom* to my son, for whom this book was written. Hopefully, when he reads it, he will gain a greater understanding of his mother, then ultimately of himself.

Contents

Introduction

It was very difficult for me to put pen in hand and begin to write this book because I had repressed so much of the core material. I had dissociated many of the events that are here recounted because I had to for the very survival of my ego. I had to will myself to remember and in the process of remembering, to relive the trauma, because I wanted to be able to describe what happened in a way that would give the reader insight into how a tragedy can alter an individual's entire personality and character make-up. In addition, I hope that chronicling such a tragic part of my life will help to heal me in some way, and in the process heal others who have gone through similar experiences. I do hope that whoever reads this work will be able to benefit from my grief in some way because it would be such a wasted experience if no one on this Earth could find something positive out of a part of my life that was so very negative.

This book is intended as a prequal to *Blind to the Molesting Hands*, where I wrote in voyeuristic detail about my relationship with Jon, a man who was just as damaged as I was, and who went on to become a misogynistic sex offender. I have no idea what he is doing now, but I have every confidence that he has been able to convince himself that all of his problems in life stem from his association with me. Because Jon was able to present such an amenable image to those in authority, the police and military establishments have never taken any of his crimes seriously. Having said that, there are few people today who take crimes committed against women seriously. As a result, Jon freely walks the streets, always in search of an unsuspecting woman to humiliate, degrade and physically harm.

Because this book is based on a time in my life before *Blind to the Molesting Hands*, it would be in the reader's interest to read that book as well so as to gain greater insight into just how bad life can get for a woman who has experienced a series of traumatic life events, but was never given any support to assimilate those experiences to enable her to heal and then go on to develop healthy relationships with others.

In the summer of 1988, I went with a friend to see a psychic. This woman had such an excellent reputation that she did not need to advertise and had a waiting list of well over six weeks. She did not speak English, so I needed a translator to understand what she was trying to say. The only thing that the psychic had difficulty with was time. She could give a reading, but she could not give an indication as to when the event would occur.

When I sat down for the reading, the first thing the clairvoyant said to me was that I would be involved in a court case and that I would lose. I could not imagine what kind of court case she could be talking about; I did not have any legal difficulties that I was aware of. I would later come to realise that the court case she spoke of was in reference to my relationship with Jon, and is chronicled in *Blind to the Molesting Hands*.

The psychic told me that I had dark blood in me, which is true. I am of Native American descent and those genes have become dominant in my make-up, as I have brown hair, brown eyes, tan skin and many of the health problems associated with Native American peoples.

I was told that I would move a lot, a point that was stressed repeatedly in the reading. I did not have any idea what she was talking about because I had just recently moved into a house and had every intention of staying there for at least three years. As it happens, I stayed in that house for almost six years. So much time had elapsed between that reading and the unfolding of events that would mark my destiny that I had come to believe the woman who had predicted my future was in fact a charlatan.

How wrong I was. Almost every word that was said to me would slowly but surely come true, but it would take over a decade for the accuracy of her predictions to become manifest.

The psychic looked at me and knew that I had a son, although I had given her no indication of the fact. The woman told me that my ex-husband was intentionally keeping me from Aaron (my son) because he wanted to punish me for what I did during our marriage. Aaron's father's family did not want me to have any contact with him because they were afraid that he would get to know me.

The reason I did not see Aaron after the end of our marriage is because my ex-husband, Enrique, had been physically violent towards me. While we were married, he broke my nose and dislocated my jaw. I know now that no woman should have to put up with that kind of battering by her husband, but such events were a sad fact of my life, being a survivor of childhood sexual, physical and mental abuse. I also blamed myself for the abuse and felt that I deserved it. I believed that I deserved to have my son taken away from me because I was such an awful person.

The reader also told me that my ex-husband liked both men and women but preferred men to women and would one day have to make a decision about his sexuality. That idea was totally new to me, but when I reflected upon her words, I recalled that my husband had never wanted me in a sexual way unless it was merely to relieve himself on me. Not once in our relationship did we ever make love; it was only sex in a highly animalistic fashion. At one point in our marriage, he told me that he did not want me in a sexual way and we abstained from sex for over a year. By the time he wanted to resume a sexual relationship with me, he had hurt me so much that I no longer desired him as a lover.

Hell is for Children

Each year in the United States, more than 3 million children are abused or neglected. The destructive experiences impact the developing child, increasing the risk of emotional, behavioural, academic, social and physical problems throughout life.

The human brain is an amazing and complex organ. It allows us to think, act, feel, laugh, speak, create and love. The brain mediates all of the qualities of humanity, good and bad. Yet the core 'mission' of the brain is to sense, perceive, process, store and act on information from the external and internal environments in the interest of survival. In order to do this, the brain has evolved an efficient and logical organisational structure.

The brain has a bottom-up organisation. The bottom regions, such as the brainstem and midbrain, control the most simple functions such as respiration, heart rate and blood pressure regulation while the top areas, which include the limbic system and cortex, control complex functions, such as thinking and regulatory emotions.

At birth, the human brain is undeveloped. Not all of the brain's areas are organised and fully functional. It is during childhood that the brain matures and a whole set of brain-related capabilities develop in a sequential fashion. We crawl before we walk; we babble before we talk.

The development of the brain during infancy and childhood follows the bottom-up structure. The most regulatory, bottom regions of the brain develop first; followed in sequence by the adjacent but higher, more complex regions.

The brain develops and modifies itself in response to experience. Neurones and synapses change in an activity-dependent fashion. Use-dependent development is the key to understanding the impact of neglect and trauma on children.

These areas organise during development and change in the mature brain in a 'use-dependent' fashion. The more a certain neural system is activated, the more it will 'build-in' this neural state – what occurs in this process is the creation of an 'internal representation' of the experience corresponding to the neural activation. This 'use-dependent' capacity to make an 'internal representation' of the external or internal world is the basis for learning and memory. The simple and unavoidable result of this sequential neurodevelopment is that the growing child is more malleable to experience than a person whose brain has matured. While experience may cause an adult to change and alter his patterns, experience literally provides the organising framework for an infant and child.

The brain is more receptive to environmental input in early childhood. The consequence of sequential development is that as different regions are organising, they require specific kinds of experience targeting the region's specific function, such as visual input while the visual system is organising, in order to develop normally. These times during development are called critical or sensitive periods.

With optimal experiences, the brain develops healthy, flexible and diverse capabilities. When there is disruption of the timing, intensity, quality or quantity of normal development experiences, however, there may be a devastating impact on neurodevelopment – and thereby on the way the brain functions. For millions of abused and neglected children, the nature of their experiences adversely influences the development of their brains. During traumatic experiences, these children's brains are in a state of fear-related activation. This activation of the neural systems in the brain leads to adaptive changes in emotional, behavioural and cognitive functioning to promote survival. Yet, persistent or chronic activation of this adaptive fear response can result in maladaptive persistence of a fear state. This activation causes hypervigilance, increased muscle tone, and focuses on threat-related cues, anxiety, behavioural impulsivity, all of which are adaptive during a threatening event yet become maladaptive when the immediate threat has passed.

This is the dilemma that traumatic abuse brings to the child's developing brain. The very process of using the proper adaptive neural response during the threat will also be the process that underlies the neural pathology, which causes so much distress and pain throughout the child's life. The chronically traumatised child will develop a host of physical signs, such as altered cardiovascular regulation, and symptoms, such as sleep and mood problems.

Some children are able to deal with abuse and neglect by developing multiple personalities or alter egos. The syndrome of multiple personality is associated with a high incidence of physical and/or sexual abuse in childhood. Multiple personality is difficult to diagnose during childhood because of the subtlety of the syndrome.

The history of dissociative disorders, which include multiple personality, extends back into New Testament times when numerous references to demon possession (a forerunner of multiple personality) were described. The phenomenon of possession continued to be prevalent until well into the 19th century and is still prevalent in certain areas of the world. However, beginning in the 18th century, the possession phenomenon began to decline and the first case of multiple personality was described by Eberhardt Gmelin in 1791. The first American case, that of Mary Reynolds, was reported in 1815. The late 19th century saw a flurry of publications about multiple personality but the relationship of multiple personality to child abuse was not generally recognised until the publication of *Sybil* in 1973.

Sybil, written by Flora Rheta Schreiber, was a true story about a woman who had 16 different personalities. The story was a number 1 best seller and over 6 million copies were sold, as well as a movie being made based on the book. *Sybil* is the story of Sybil Isabel Dorsett who was diagnosed as having a multiple personality disorder. Dr Wilber, her psychiatrist, diagnoses her with this disorder and reported 16 other 'selves'. It is widely speculated that Dr Wilbur had compromised her situation as a psychiatrist by manipulating the main character, Sybil. What is amazing is that Dr Wilbur mapped the hierarchy of Sybil's 16 'selves'. Five of these personalities were very similar and were direct descendants from Sybil's true personality. From the main personalities, others were derived, and two such descendant personalities were even male.

It seems that Sybil, in an attempt to cope with the rather traumatic abuses perpetrated by her very eccentric parents, developed a way to survive the ordeal without having to remember. During each assault, a personality that was a derivative of her core personality would come through and take the abuse for her. This mental strategy enabled her core 'self' to mature and develop the best way she could under the circumstances, and become an adult who had very little conscious recollection of her rather traumatic childhood.

Multiple personality most often presents with depression and suicidality rather than personality changes, and amnesia, which are obvious clues to dissociation. The amnesia in multiple personality includes amnesia for traumatic experiences in the remote past and amnesia for recent events that occurred while the individual was dissociated into another personality. Often, emotional stress precipitates dissociation. The amnesiac episodes generally last from a few minutes to a few hours but occasionally may last from a few days to a few months. The original personality is usually amnesiac for the secondary personalities while the secondary personalities may have varying awareness of one another. Sometimes, a secondary personality may exhibit the phenomenon of co-consciousness and be aware of events even when another personality is dominant. Generally, the original personality is rather reserved and depleted of affect. The secondary personalities usually express affects or impulses unacceptable to the primary personality, such as anger, depression or sexuality. Differences between personalities may be quite subtle or striking. Personalities may be of a different age, race, sex, sexual orientation, or parentage from the original. Most often, the personalities have chosen proper names for themselves. Psychophysiological symptoms are frequent in multiple personality. Headaches are also common as are hysterical conversion symptoms and symptoms of sexual dysfunction.

Transient psychotic episodes may occur in multiple personality. Hallucinations during such episodes are usually of a complex visual nature indicating a hysterical type of psychosis. Sometimes, a personality will hear the voices of other personalities. These voices, which occasionally are of a command type, appear to come from inside the head, and should not be confused with the auditory hallucinations of schizophrenia, which usually come from outside the head. Most often, stress precipitates the transition between personalities. These transitions may be dramatic or quite subtle.

The onset of multiple personality generally occurs in childhood, although the condition is not usually diagnosed until adolescence or early adulthood. About 85 per cent of multiple personality sufferers are women. This increased incidence of multiple personality in women may occur because sexual abuse and incest, which are strongly associated with multiple personality, occur predominantly in female children and adolescents. The degree of impairment in multiple personality may vary from mild to severe.

Trauma has long been recognised as an essential criterion for the production of dissociate disorders including multiple personality. The various types of trauma include childhood physical and sexual abuse, rape, combat, natural disasters, accidents, concentration camp experiences, loss of loved ones, financial catastrophes, and severe marital discord. As early as 1896, Sigmund Freud recognised that early childhood seduction experiences were responsible for 18 cases of hysteria, a condition closely associated with dissociative disorders.

It was not until the publication of *Sybil* in 1973 that childhood physical and sexual abuse became widely recognised as precipitants of multiple personality. Since 1973, numerous investigations have confirmed the high incidence of physical and sexual abuse in multiple personality.

The types of child abuse experienced by victims of multiple personality are quite varied. Sexual abuses include incest, rape, sexual molestation, sodomy, cutting of the sexual organs and inserting objects into the sexual organs. Physical abuses include cutting, bruising, beating, hanging, tying up, and being locked in closets and cellars. Neglect and verbal abuse are also common.

The abuse in multiple personality is usually severe, prolonged and perpetrated by family members who are bound to the child in a love–hate relationship.

In the childhood form of multiple personality, the differences between personalities are quite subtle, and the number of personalities is fewer. An average of four personalities has been reported in children, while the average of personalities reported in adults is 13. Symptoms of depression and somatic complaints are less common in children but the symptoms of amnesia and inner voices are not decreased. Symptoms characteristic of childhood multiple personality disorder include:

1. A history of repeated child abuse.
2. Subtle alternating personality changes such as a shy child with depressed, angry, seductive and/or regressive episodes.

3. Amnesia of abuse and/or other recent events, such as schoolwork, angry outbursts, regressive behaviour.
4. Marked variations in abilities such as schoolwork, games and music.
5. Trance-like states.
6. Disavowed behaviour leading to being called a liar.

As is the case with child abuse (particularly incest), there is a professional reluctance to diagnose multiple personality disorder. In all likelihood, this reluctance stems from a number of factors including the generally subtle presentation of the symptoms, the fearful reluctance of the patient to divulge important clinical information, professional ignorance concerning dissociative disorders and the reluctance of the clinician to believe that incest actually occurs and is not the product of fantasy.

If the patient with multiple personality presents with depression and suicidality and if the differences between personalities are subtle, the diagnosis may be missed. The changes in personality may be attributed to a simple mood change, for instance. In other cases, the individuals with multiple personality may go through prolonged periods without dissociation, and therefore the diagnosis is missed because a 'window of diagnosibility' did not exist at the time of the clinical examination.

In addition to the subtle presentation of multiple personality, most individuals with this disorder consciously withhold vital clinical information about memory loss, hallucinations and knowledge of other personalities in order to avoid being labelled crazy. Others withhold information out of distrust. Still others are totally unaware that they are symptomatic. For instance, they may be completely unaware of alter personalities, and the time loss or time distortion they experience may have occurred for such a long time that they consider it normal.

The reluctance of the clinician to believe that incest occurs or has occurred in their patients is perhaps the most troubling aspect regarding the misdiagnosis of multiple personality. In many cases, stories of incest have been assumed to be fantasies or outright lies. The practice of non-belief has occurred despite cases in which sexual abuse has been carefully confirmed with collateral sources. This problem of clinician disbelief is thought to be a counter transference reaction to the traumatised victim.

Undoubtedly, Freud's renunciation of his earlier belief in the seduction theory was a setback to understanding incest. For many years after Freud's renunciation, clinicians assumed stories of incest to be fantasy. The counter transference reactions to victims' traumatic abuse included extreme anxiety about the abuse and resultant avoidance of the topic, a conspiracy to maintain silence about the abuse, and blaming the victim for abuse. The clinician's incredulity regarding the abuse functions to make him or her believe that the patient and her family are not as sick as they seem, hence the uncomfortable obligation of having to report abuse or appear in court is unnecessary. Disbelief shields the clinician from the powerful rage expressed by the victim and her family if confrontation about the abuse occurs.

The psychiatric syndrome of multiple personality is associated with an extremely high incidence of physical and/or sexual abuse during childhood. The abuse is usually severe, prolonged, and perpetrated by family members. Multiple personality may be difficult to diagnose because of the subtlety of the presenting symptoms, the patient's fear of being labelled crazy and the clinician's mistaken belief that multiple personality is a rare condition. Currently, multiple personality is usually diagnosed in adults who are in their late 20's or early 30's. The diagnosis of multiple personality in children is more difficult because of the subtlety of symptoms and the ease with which these symptoms are confused with fantasy. Although individuals with multiple personality do not usually abuse their own children, the incidence of psychiatric disturbance in their children is high.

Because abuse and neglect cause a great deal of psychological disturbance in children and continue well into adulthood, it would be wise for the individual to become well informed about child abuse and neglect.

One may abuse or neglect a child by inflicting harm or by failing to act to prevent harm. Children may be abused in a family or in an institutional or community setting; by those known to them or, more rarely, by a stranger.

Physical abuse may involve hitting, shaking, throwing, poisoning, burning or scalding, drowning, suffocating or otherwise causing physical harm to a child. Physical harm may also be caused when a parent or carer feigns the symptoms or deliberately causes ill health to a child they are looking after. This situation is commonly described using terms such as factitious illness by proxy or Munchausen's Syndrome by proxy.

Emotional abuse is the persistent emotional ill treatment of a child such as to delay the child's emotional development. It may involve conveying to children that they are worthless or unloved, inadequate, or valued only insofar as they meet the needs of another person. It may feature age or developmentally inappropriate expectations being imposed on children. It may involve causing children frequently to feel frightened or in danger, or the exploitation or corruption of children. Some level of emotional abuse is involved in all types of ill treatment of a child, though it may occur alone.

Sexual abuse involves forcing or enticing a child or young person to take part in sexual activities whether or not the child is aware of what is happening. The activities may involve physical contact, including penetration (rape or buggery) or non-penetrative acts. They may include non-contact activities, such as involving children in looking at, or in the production of, pornographic material or watching sexual activities, or encouraging children to behave in sexually inappropriate ways.

Neglect is the persistent failure to meet a child's basic physical and/or psychological needs, likely to result in serious impairment of the child's health or development. It may involve a parent or carer failing to provide adequate food, shelter and clothing, failing to protect a child from physical harm or danger, or the failure to ensure access to appropriate medical care or treatment. It may include neglect of, or unresponsiveness to, a child's basic emotional needs.

Children may suffer more than one form of abuse. It should also be remembered that the abuse may be caused by persons other than the carers or parents, e.g., relatives, family friends, babysitter, sibling or stranger. There may be abuse at school, in a residential establishment or a foster home.

Injurious physical abuse should not be ignored. The explanation (or lack of explanation) by the parent or carer should be examined and one should be alert to a change of explanation. Repeated injuries need to be treated with caution. Bruises or weals may occur on the face, ears, head, torso or multiple body places. Bruises can occur on the legs before a child is mobile. Bruising can occur on the wrists or ankles as a result of swinging; black eyes without bruising on the forehead is another sign of abuse. Bruising from fingertips or from bites may occur. Bruises in various stages of healing or clusters that form regular patterns, such as the shape of an article, are grounds for suspicion. Bruising may also occur regularly after weekends, school absences or holidays.

Children who are being abused physically show various behaviour indicators that are different from a child who has not been abused. These indicators are:

- The child is wary of physical contact by parents/carers or others.
- The child does not look to the parent for reassurance.
- The child cries hopelessly under examination or treatment.

* The child shows no expectations of being comforted, and cries little in general.
* The child seems less afraid than other children and settles in quickly when admitted to the hospital ward.
* The child constantly asks in words or actions what will happen next.
* The child will ask when he is going home or announce that he is not going home, rather than cry that he wants to go home.

Munchausen's (Meadow's) Syndrome by proxy (factitious illness syndrome) occurs when parents, usually the mother, systematically provide fictitious information about their child's symptoms or attempt to tamper with an investigation. The child may be submitted to innumerable investigations and medical interventions. Eventually, the child may suffer illness, be permanently handicapped or even die.

When parents emotionally abuse their children, they behave in very specific ways which can involve acts of commission or omission. The main characteristic is that it consists of persistent and pervasive types of behaviour.

1. Rejecting involves active expressions of rejection (as opposed to passively ignoring a child) such as scapegoating or actively refusing to help a child.
2. Degrading is action that deprecates the child, including verbal derogation, such as insulting or publicly humiliating.
3. Terrorising is actions or threats that cause a child extreme fear and anxiety, such as threatening to hurt or kill, or leaving a child unattended.
4. Isolating is actions that separate the child from others, such as locking children in closets or in a room alone and refusing to allow interactions with others outside the family.

5. Mis-socialising, also called corrupting, is acts that render the child antisocial or mis-socialised, that teach or otherwise encourage the child to develop orientations that are destructive to others or himself, such as encouraging criminal behaviour or substance abuse by the child, or inculcating racist values.

6. Exploiting is situations in which a child is used for advantage or profit, such as sexual molestation, treating the child as a servant or surrogate parent, using the child for the purpose of pornography or prostitution, involving the child inappropriately in the adult conflict when parents are separated.

7. Denying emotional responsiveness is acts of omission in which the caregiver fails to provide the sensitive, responsive caregiving necessary to development. The caregiver is detached, uninvolved, and interacts with the child only when necessary.

8. Marital violence involves bitter disputes between parents.

Children who are being emotionally abused will exhibit very specific behavioural indicators. They will:

- Exhibit habit disorders, such as sucking, rocking and biting.
- Display conduct disorders, such as antisocial or destructive behaviour.
- Experience sleep disorders.
- Be compliant/passive, aggressive/demanding, or hyperactive.
- Display developmental lags.
- Have problems with wetting or soiling.
- Display excessively adaptive behaviour.
- Show signs of role reversal, such as the child's taking on responsibility that his parents should be fulfilling.
- Exhibit frozen watchfulness, which is when a child has a glazed expression, is wide eyed and very still.

Acts of omission can be understood as the absence of positive parenting behaviour, such as:

- Physical care and affection.
- Emotional warmth and approval.
- Stimulation and teaching.
- Opportunity and encouragement to acquire autonomy gradually.
- Discipline and control.

Neglect is also a form of abuse because the parents or carers are not ensuring the child's basic needs are being met:

- The child fails to thrive.
- The child has bad hygiene.
- Prescriptions are not collected.
- Immunisations are incomplete.
- The child is not adequately protected.
- Appropriate health care is not given.
- Health advice is not heeded.
- Missed appointments.
- Children are not safely supervised.
- Poor school attendance.
- Deficient parental attendance.
- Failure to protect the child from serious injury from older siblings.
- Lack of provision for leisure and play.
- Inadequate or inappropriate clothing.
- An unsafe or unhygienic home.

Children may also be sexually abused. The physical signs of such abuse are injuries to the genital area or anus, pain in the genital area: itching, bleeding, bruising, discharge. Difficulties in walking and sitting. Repeated urinary infections, sexually trans-mitted disease, persistent sore throats, pregnancy in teenagers, eating disorders, self-mutilation.

When a child is sexually abused, he will behave in ways differ-ent from non-abused children. He or she will exhibit:

◆ Regressive behaviour/attainment.
◆ Aggressive/sexualised behaviour to other children.
◆ Sexual promiscuity.
◆ Inappropriate sexually provocative behaviour for age.
◆ Inappropriate displays of affection.
◆ Secrets, fantasies.
◆ Emotionally isolated, poor self-image.
◆ Lack of peer relationships. Sleep disturbances. Acute anxiety/fear.
◆ Refusal to go to school.
◆ Running away from home.
◆ Suicide attempts.
◆ Obsessive washing.
◆ Drawing, stories.

Some children are more susceptible to abuse than others.

Children who are born too soon are particularly vulnerable because they are born before parents are emotionally ready for them. They are statistically more likely to have been born prema-turely, with lower weight, vulnerable to ill health. As a result, they will be difficult to handle and a cause of anxiety.

Children who are born sick or handicapped are at risk of abuse. The mother could have had an abnormal pregnancy, abnormal labour or delivery, neonatal separation, or other illness in the first year of life.

If a child is born who is different from what his parents wanted, this will make him vulnerable to abuse.

Unwanted children are particularly vulnerable to abuse. The pregnancy could have been unwanted, the gender of the child could be not what the parents were hoping for, or the actual child could be a disappointing replacement for the loss of a previous child or someone precious.

The parents could have issues of their own, which would make them particularly susceptible to abusing children. They could have low self-esteem, too much life stress, be physically violent, or have fragile relationships. The parents may expect criticism or rejection, or resent authority.

A family's particular circumstances will predispose it to abuse. Stress can be a very important factor in triggering child abuse, e.g., poor housing, moving house, unemployment, low income, depression, pregnancy or a new baby or bereavement. Several stress factors occurring within a short period of time can cause breakdown in otherwise competent and loving families.

Stressful circumstances may be particularly important when:

♦ The family lacks a lifeline in the form of a supportive extended family or friends, and there is no one available to give practical help and understanding.
♦ The family has moved several times and there are no local roots.
♦ There is a known history of previously unexplained or inadequately explained injuries, or of previous known abuse of children in the family.
♦ An adult member of the household has previously been responsible for child abuse in another household.

***

To be perfectly honest, it was not until I was almost 40 years old that I had any idea that I had been abused. I honestly believed that all people treated their children the way that I had been treated as a child. Perhaps if I had been brought up in a home where there was a little bit of love and understanding, my life would not have turned out to be such a tragedy. Perhaps if I had been treated with a bit of decency and respect as a child, I might have wanted to have children of my own.

Instead, since I had been abused so badly during my more formative years, I went on to form relationships with men who would use and abuse me in the same way that my parents and carers had done.

I was born prematurely on 30th January 1961, an unwanted twin. I weighed in at 4½ pounds and my sister, one pound heavier, was called 'the big one'. Technically underweight, I already had a disadvantaged start to life because statistics have shown that low birth-weight babies tend developmentally to lag behind normal weight babies.

My mother did not want any babies, and at the age of 18 she already had three! She was a prime candidate as an abusive mother because she had been abused and neglected by both of her parents. Perhaps if she had had a better upbringing, she would not have found herself 16 and pregnant. To make matters worse, she did not get any support from her own family, which further intensified her feelings of isolation, inadequacy and shame.

I was born in Little Rock, Arkansas, the centre of the Bible Belt. As far as I can tell, the only thing that fundamentalist religions have done is to harm women and children as well as create wars and strife. The Bible propagates child abuse, and one of the most well-known biblical phrases is 'spare the rod and spoil the child'. Many an adult has used the Bible as an excuse to inflict physical harm on a vulnerable child.

Another biblical favourite is the fourth commandment, which states, 'Thou shalt honour thy father and mother.' That one little commandment has kept many a child in line if his parents ever suspected he might be on the verge of revealing to others what went on at home.

If people were okay with themselves, they would know in their heart what correct and acceptable behaviour is. They would not need another individual to tell them.

The first time I almost came to an early demise was when I was only two weeks old, which would have been in February, 1961. Apparently my father, Matthew, was bored and decided to take the family out to the country where his parents live. The fact that it was raining heavily was of no consequence to my father, who rarely ever thought of anyone other than himself.

While driving along a gravel road, he somehow managed to leave the road and land the car in a large body of water. Like most men, he chose to save himself before thinking of anyone else. He took my brother, Marc, and swam with him to dry ground where he would be safe. My father left my mother holding her two premature babies, sitting inside a flooded car.

Matthew called to my mother and told her that he was going to get help.

'Don't leave me here!' my mother called to my father.

'I can't leave Marc,' Matthew called back. 'If I go into the water, Marc will follow me!'

'Take your belt off and tie Marc to a tree!' my mother implored.

But it was too late. Matthew was already gone. My mother sat in that flooded car, holding one twin in each arm. She very well could have saved herself and left my sister and me to drown. Nobody in rural Arkansas would have asked any questions or held it against her if she had abandoned us and swum to safety. My mother might indeed have gone ahead and done so, were it not for the fact that she couldn't swim.

Although my mother wanted desperately to be rid of her two unwanted girls, I believe that something inside her held her back from allowing them to drown. My mother's almost non-existent maternal instincts kicked in, and on probably the only occasion in her life, she put the needs of her children before her own.

My mother waited, and waited, and waited, hoping that a miracle would happen and she would be rescued. On that cold, winter night a miracle did in fact occur.

A group of young men, probably the same age as my mother, were out joyriding on that lonely road on the outskirts of Little Rock. When my mother saw the headlights approaching her, she used her foot to push the horn of the car. The horn blared, and blared, and blared until the young men got out of the car and investigated the situation. My mother called the young men to come and get her and the twins out of the car. One has to wonder what the odds were that a group of teenage boys would decide to go for a joyride in the Arkansas countryside on that particular cold, rainy night. I don't even know the name of the young men who saved my life.

Nothing was ever said to my father about why he drove so dangerously that he put his car into a large body of water. Nothing was ever said to my father about why he left the scene of the accident. I doubt very seriously that anyone would have been concerned in the least if I had met an untimely demise on that cold, winter night. Lest one think I have made this story up to elicit sympathy, my mother told me the event was reported in the local papers, hence the seriousness of the situation. I suppose that destiny was at work on that night and other nights afterwards. I really should not have lived to tell this tale, but somehow I did.

The second time I almost came to an early death was when I was about three years old. Ostensibly, I had been bitten by a dog, but the resulting scar resembled that of a knife wound and not of a dog's teeth. The attack left me with an incision above my left eye below the brow. I have seen pictures of children who have been bitten in the face by dogs and it is normally the cheeks that are affected. In retrospect, I suppose that I wasn't really bitten by a dog because the resulting scar would have been much more horrific.

My mother, a pathological liar, made up a story of how I had put a Halloween mask on a dog and it had responded by biting me in the eye. I don't think my mother was ever really able to look at me after she attacked me in such a brutal way. Every time she tried to look me in the eye she would have seen her handiwork. While my mother could lie to other people, she could never lie to herself, so the emotional distance between us became even wider.

In addition to the fact that my father almost killed me when I was only two weeks old, my parents also adopted a more subtle approach by slowly killing me little by little each and every day. My sister and I rarely, if ever, were fed properly. If it were not for the fact that I have an incredibly slow metabolism and can survive on almost nothing, I surely would have starved to death. So malnourished were my sister and I that my grandmother told me we would eat dirt. A lot of people don't know this, but soil has a lot of valuable nutrients in it. I can only suppose that my will to live kicked in and I ate dirt as a survival mechanism.

When I was older, my mother would tell a tale that she made meatloaf for me when I was a baby. Even as I child, I never had any recollection of my mother's ever making me any meal, much less meatloaf. I would just look at my mother blankly and try to remember eating the meatloaf that she claimed to have made, but I couldn't. I have very little memory of my mother's ever giving me any food to eat before the age of eight.

My mother also said she gave my sister and me a piece of candy each and every day. Again, I have no recollection whatsoever of my mother's ever giving me any candy to eat.

I never refuted the family myth that my mother was a caring person who doted on me and made me meatloaf for dinner. If my mother said it was so, it must have been. Who was I to contradict her?

Not only did my parents not feed me, they denied both my sister and myself any physical contact. Because my sister and I were unwanted, our parents gave us almost no physical contact whatsoever. They never picked us up or cuddled us like most parents do, but just left us in our cot, leaving us to our own devices. If it were not for the fact that we had each other, we might very well have died. It is a well-known fact that babies who are not touched will die, so it is something of a miracle that my sister and I survived. Somehow we lived through it all, but we certainly did not thrive.

Because my sister and I did not have anyone but each other, we would rock ourselves to sleep, the rhythmic motion helping us to drop off into a hungry slumber.

My grandmother said that in addition to the rocking, we would not utter a word. We would quietly moan to each other while we rocked back and forth. We had each other for company. We were our own best friends. If we did not have each other, we probably would have died from neglect.

The innocent bystander would be inclined to assume that my sister and I were autistic because we exhibited signs of the ailment. We were not autistic, however, just severely neglected.

I can recall when I was a pre-schooler, I went to my grandmother while she sat on her big lazy boy lounger. I told her that I had killed a person. My grandmother chastised me and told me to never say such things again. I have no idea why I would make such a declaration to my grandmother when I was no more than three or four years of age. I have since learned that children who are abused will often say they have killed a baby.

When we were old enough to fix our own meals, our chances of physical survival greatly improved. It was at that point that our mother stopped preparing meals for us altogether, if she ever did in the first place. Because we had to fix food that was simple for a child to prepare, our diet consisted primarily of corn flakes for breakfast and a baloney sandwich for lunch. Hardly a balanced diet, but it was enough food to allow us to survive.

When I was six years old and started school, my mother sat me down and told me that it was my responsibility to get up every morning and walk down to the bus stop so I could get to school. Even though I didn't have a clock, somehow I managed to get dressed and walk down to the bus stop every day, thereby allowing my mother to stay asleep in her bed.

When I got older, my mother was finally able to find a practical use for her daughters: free labour. When she discovered that we could be taught how to clean the house, she never again lifted a finger in it. Every evening, we washed the dishes and did the laundry. On Saturday, we would clean the house from top to bottom, and on Sunday morning we were obliged to clean the house all over again after a wild night of socialising. My mother saw her daughters as her own personal slaves who would clean her house and work in her beauty shop for no recompense whatsoever.

My mother took particular pleasure in verbally abusing me. She said that I was dirty and lazy, and would berate me for the most minor transgressions. I remember quite vividly one autumn day when I was in the 4th grade. Out of the blue, my mother barked at me that she did not want me and my father did not want me, but that she was stuck with me. There was not much I could say after that little declaration, so I just said nothing. To be honest, I rarely ever replied to my mother's outbursts. If I retorted, it would only bring more abuse. If I said nothing, however, maybe she would tire of the abuse and stop.

While I was still in the 4th grade, my mother derisively told my sister that I was warped. I have no doubt she expressed those sentiments to other family members because years later, my brother's wife at the time informed me that I had a 'warped perspective' when we were merely having an innocent conversation about university education.

When I was 13 or 14 years old, my mother came home quite abruptly from one of her many nights out on the town. My sister squealed about something insignificant and my mother screamed at her that she was a 'fucking bitch'. There was not much that either of us could say after our mother had called us such offensive names. It was very difficult for us to establish any kind of decent rapport when the only things that she could say to us were derisive in nature.

My mother also failed to protect me from harm. She worked as a hairdresser, owned her own beauty shop and was a pretty successful businesswoman in Little Rock. I was being bullied at school by the daughters of one of her customers. Instead of my mother doing the decent thing and telling the bully's mother that she would have to find another hairdresser as long as her daughter was behaving in a threatening way, she continued to cut the woman's hair without a care in the world about how I felt.

My mother was unconcerned that I could not even use the toilet at school because that is where the local bullies hung out. Her only concern was for herself and she was not prepared to put forth the slightest bit of effort to protect her child.

For reasons I do not understand, my mother took a dislike to my friends. When I was in the 7th grade, I had two friends in particular, and my mother took a dislike to them even though she had never met them. She actually went to great lengths to tell me not to play with them and to find other friends. She was never able to give me an adequate explanation as to why she did not want me to be friends with Linda and Sherry, so I stayed friends with them without my mother's consent or approval. It was probably at that time that I stopped speaking to my mother about my friends because she was so critical of me and of everything I did.

A couple of years later, my friend Linda telephoned me and told me that her brother, who was gay, had told her that my mother was heavily involved in the lesbian and gay scene in Little Rock and was involved in a lesbian relationship with her 'friend' Bobbie. Although I was shocked at the revelation, I was not surprised. For as long as I can remember, my mother had had really intense relationships with other women.

I can only assume that the mothers in Little Rock did not want their children playing with me because they somehow felt my mother's sexual orientation would rub off. It is possible that the mothers in question telephoned my mother and said some unkind things to her, which resulted in her trying to dictate to me whom I would and would not be friends with.

Although my mother is not a particularly clean or hygienic person, she decided to project the uncleanness that she felt within herself onto her children. She and my stepfather, Bill, constantly told me and my sister that we were dirty. When we lived with our grandmother, we were only allowed to bathe once a week to save water; therefore, when we went back to live with our mother, we continued that practice. My mother never once informed us that there was plenty of water and we could bathe as often as we liked, but instead told us every day how dirty we were. Bill, who was a teacher and should have known better, got on the bandwagon as well and parroted my mother's sentiments.

When I reached adolescence, I had an iron deficiency and was plagued with sties and boils. Instead of my mother's taking me to a doctor, she said that I got boils because I was dirty.

My mother needed very little provocation to become hysterical. She would decide out of the blue that we would have to clean the feet of all the chairs and stools in the house. Whenever I tried to speak to her about being able to go out with boys or driving a car, she would become so hysterical that it was pointless speaking to her. When I left the room in anger, she would usually throw something at me.

My mother was also quite a sadist, a trait my sister no doubt picked up from her. My earliest memory of my mother was of her and her second husband, Bob, giving us onions to eat. Mama and Bob both giggled to each other as we naïvely sank our teeth into the very sharp bulbs. I must say that my mother's actions were certainly not those of a loving, caring person.

The abuse and neglect my sister and I both suffered at her

hands was no doubt related to her inherent sadism. For reasons that I will never understand, my mother actually enjoyed harming her children. I would like to point out that she had been abused too, and if she had not been abused, neglected and rejected herself, she might very well have grown up to be a loving and caring person. Sadly, that was not the case.

I was also sexually abused. Because the very survival of my personality meant that it must fragment into various sub-personalities, I have little conscious recollection of the more sinister acts that were committed against me. Instead, I have pictorial flashes that come to me from time to time, usually when I least expect it. What normally happens is that a rather mundane event will trigger a flashback and I will have the displeasure of experiencing the event all over again.

The earliest memories I have are of sitting in the chair with my grandfather. I must have been no more than three or four years old, but was trying to move my grandfather's fingers down, so that they formed the obscene 'bird' sign, and it goes without saying that 'flipping the bird' is a very vulgar act indeed. Even at that young age I knew that the hand sign I was trying to make was a very naughty thing to do, but I tried to do it nonetheless. I have no idea who taught me that hand gesture – I only know that I knew it was considered very naughty and wanted my grandfather to form that hand sign as an act of naughtiness.

I also have body memories of someone taking me by force and doing with me whatever he liked. I have no memories other than that, except for the fact that my carers knew very well what was going on and turned a blind eye to it.

I suppose that I loved my father very much because he was a very illusive, unavailable figure. I recall that he would take my sister into the bedroom so that he could give her a spanking and would spend time inside the room alone with her. Years later, when I asked my sister about what they did in the room, she said she had no recollection of him ever taking her in a room and spending time with her alone. It is important at this point to note that my grandmother knew very well that my father was taking his young daughter into rooms and spending time alone with them. I cannot recall my grandmother's ever expressing any objections to my father's behaviour, so in that respect at least, my grandmother failed to protect my sister from any inappropriate behaviour that may have taken place.

Even my stepfather got in on the act. One Sunday morning when, I can only assume, his sexual advances towards my mother had been spurned, he entered the bedroom I shared with my sister. I was not in the room, but my sister was, and he stayed alone with her in that room for quite some time. When I was finally allowed to go back into the bedroom, my sister was huddled in the corner with tears streaming down her face. When I asked my sister what the matter was, she said that my stepfather was going to give her a spanking because the room was dirty. Years later, when I asked my sister about that incident, she had no recollection of it.

My sister and I made perfect incest victims. Our mother was never at home to protect us because she was out cruising the bars in Little Rock every night of the week. Her excuse for her behaviour was that she had to give up her childhood for her children, so she was going to go out and relive her childhood. What she failed to realise was that her two daughters did not have much of a childhood either because of her lifestyle and behaviour.

My sister and I were responsible for all the household chores. We had virtually taken over our mother's role in the house, not because we wanted to, but because we were forced to. Because my mother was never home, I can only assume that my stepfather decided to get revenge on my mother and satisfy his sexual needs all in one go.

I went through a phase where I did not want to sleep in the same bed with my sister, so I would sleep on the couch in the parlour adjacent to the room I shared with my sister. I have fleeting memories of my stepfather's entering the room where I slept, but nothing else.

One Saturday evening, when my mother was out cruising the bars, my stepfather actually started flirting with and took an undue interest in me. I was very nervous, to say the least. This was a man who had never shown any interest in me at all, had called me names and behaved derisively towards me. Once I began looking more like a woman, he began treating me with more interest. I did not respond to my stepfather's advances and have no recollection of any inappropriate behaviour, but the incident left me unnerved nonetheless.

Years later, when my sister had children of her own and left them in the care of my mother, her lesbian lover, and my stepfather, I shuddered. I did not think that my niece should be left in the care of my stepfather and told her so. My sister, having blocked out memories of her own abuse, dismissed my concerns. My niece was therefore left in the care of highly unsuitable individuals, thus replicating the familiar cycle of abuse that I am all too aware of.

My mother also allowed her lesbian lovers to corrupt her daughters. When I was 13, I recall vividly Bobbie, my mother's latest paramour, taking us to a drive-in pornographic movie. I was too embarrassed to watch it, but there was something wrong with my mother's mind to allow her two adolescent girls to watch obscene acts with her and her girlfriend. I know now that what my mother and her girlfriend did is classified as corrupting.

Bobbie, my mother's lesbian lover at the time, also earned a little extra money by working as a prostitute. I have no doubt that she did anything and everything her clients asked of her because while only in her early 30s, she already had a bad case of haemorrhoids and needed surgery to rectify the situation. I can only assume that she developed haemorrhoids because she would submit to anal sex if the price was right.

Bobbie and Mama would drop my sister and me off at the

movies and stay away for hours. When the movies were over, my sister and I would stand out in the dark waiting for our mother to come collect us. My mother and Bobbie never explained where they had been and what they had been doing, and I never asked.

Bobbie would also invite me to spend Saturday nights at her house. We would all sleep in her bed together and I thought it was totally innocent. The visits eventually took on a more sinister tone, however.

Bobbie and Mama were both obsessed with sex and kept pornography in their homes. I can only assume that their promiscuous and lewd sexual behaviour was a result of their own experiences of childhood abuse, but their behaviour was certainly not a positive influence on young minds. In addition to the pornography, my mother also owned sex toys that she did not even bother to hide. Because sex was such a large part of our day to day lives, I was merely amused to discover the full extent of my mother's sex life.

Not surprisingly, by the time I was a teenager I had developed an angry sub-personality. It did not come out very often, but I would sometimes find myself lashing out at other people.

When I was in the 8th grade, the angry me seemed to be the most prominent. On two occasions in particular, my teachers told me that I was not very ladylike and that I should not be so harsh with other people.

Again, when I was 16, an angry personality again began to emerge, and I feel that it was a result of the fact that my brother was seriously ill in the hospital, my mother was never home and, although I have no recollection of it, something inappropriate may have been going on with my stepfather. I was very angry with my mother and it was difficult for me to conceal the animosity I felt towards her.

In retrospect, the angry me seems out of character with the person I am today. I would never dream of hurting another person and will normally refrain from speaking my mind if my views are going to upset anyone else. If anything, as an adult I am quite withdrawn, so when I look back at the angry personality that emerged from time to time, I am quite bemused. It is not enough for me to say that I am ashamed of the way I behaved during those times: I can only say that the angry me was quite out of character with who I really am.

I think that death and tragic accidents tend to change a family forever. There is an old saying, 'That which doesn't kill, makes us stronger', and I can think of nothing more eloquently meaningful than that one phrase. When we encounter difficulties, what do we do? Do we face them and let the chips fly where they may, or do we hide our heads in the sand and hope they will go away if we ignore them long enough? For such a long time, we were five planets existing in that galaxy that we tried to call a home, and it was only a matter of time before cataclysm would change things forever. Because there were no controls in our family, a quickening occurred and none of us were the same afterwards.

One morning in May 1977, I left for school as usual. It was a warm, sunny day and I could foresee nothing out of the ordinary transpiring. When I came home from school, however, I was ushered to the hospital and informed that my brother had been involved in a motorcycle accident and was lying in intensive care.

To make matters worse, I was not asked, but told, that I would be giving blood to save his life. Of course I did not want my brother to die. I would have given anything in the world for him to live through what had happened. But my mother, in her massive neglect of her children, had not noticed that I had a profound phobia of needles and other sharp objects. I almost needed to be in intensive care myself when I was told that some strange person was going to stick a needle in me and take my blood.

Of course I would do it. I couldn't let my brother die just because I was afraid of needles. Fortunately for me, while my mother was busy calculating how many pints of blood she could get out of my body so that she would not have to pay for any, someone in authority came and informed her that since I was not yet 17 years of age, they were not legally allowed to subject me to something so traumatic.

One of my aunts later told me that on that evening in the waiting room, Bobbie was all over Mama, holding her hand and telling her how much she loved her. It was sickening, really. Even when we had a serious family incident and my brother could very well have died, Bobbie was in the thick of it, vying for my mother's attention.

That day was a whirlwind for me because I did not really comprehend what was happening. My brother and I have never had a good rapport. Just a few months prior to his accident, we had a massive argument over something trivial. He blocked my way and would not let me pass. Along with hitting him and screaming at him, I told him that I wished that he would die. Of course, I scarcely imagined that such a thing could happen, but as I stood in the waiting room of the hospital that day, I had to take careful stock of the things that I had said to him in anger.

Little by little, I was able to listen to people and piece together the events of the day. It appears that Marc woke up late so, in a hurry, he sped down the road so as not to be late to school. The road we lived on was hilly with curves and bends, and if one weren't careful, it was easy to have an accident. On this particular day, an employee of the state was operating a tractor, performing road works. He had not placed any signs on the road stating that road works were in progress, so my brother had no way of knowing that there was an obstruction at the bottom of the hill as he sped down Colonel Glenn Road. When he reached the bottom of the hill and saw the massive tractor blocking the road, it was too late for him to take evasive action. His motorcycle hit the tractor, he flew into the air and landed on the ground some distance away. When he regained consciousness, he saw that his leg was very badly broken.

Unfortunately, the man who was operating the tractor must have had some problems himself because instead of going to the nearest telephone and calling for an ambulance, he merely sat by the tractor berating my brother. One of the neighbours saw the accident and went to tell my mother what had happened. When my mother arrived at the scene, an ambulance was called but it took almost three-quarters of an hour to arrive. My mother, not knowing just how serious the situation was, took her time trying to find a good surgeon, thus bringing my brother even closer to death's door. The surgeons operated, but Marc would have to endure many more procedures over an extensive healing process before he could leave that hospital – a man changed forever.

My mother was absolutely devastated by what had happened to Marc and became the devoted mother that she should have been during the initial 17 years of his life. She was at the hospital day and night. It seemed that she could not do enough for her son, and even he had to ask her not to pet him so much, as he simply wasn't used to being pampered and coddled.

Mama took me to the hospital to see my brother once, which I found to be an uncomfortable experience. Although he was my brother, in reality he was a strange person with whom I lived but did not really know at all. I sat next to the hospital bed, trying to act normal as I watched my brother, drugged up on painkillers, trying to make conversation with me. I am so ashamed to say that I was relieved when I was allowed to go home.

I now know that my mother was working through her own illness, which involved seeking attention whilst in hospital, by staying close to Marc during his recuperation. Mama's doting had less to do with love for her son than her own fascination with hospitals and the attention she derived from being in them.

Although I didn't know it at the time, my mother was so chintzy that she had let the insurance for my brother lapse. Although my mother openly felt that her children should take responsibility for looking after themselves, the law thought otherwise. Since my brother was not yet 18 at the time of the accident, she was faced with a massive hospital bill. I have no doubt that my mother would have told my brother to pay the hospital bill himself if he were not so close to death. I honestly think that my mother is such a selfish person that she could cope much more easily with the loss of a child than financial ruin because she lost me when I was 16 and didn't bat an eyelash.

During the summer, when my brother was still in the hospital, I had become increasingly disgusted with my mother. The respect was all gone and I didn't even try to hide my contempt for her any more.

One thing I did not know, however, was the fact that Mama's good friend Bobbie had been stealing from her. With all of my mother's financial concerns, she must have discovered that some of her money was missing. She discussed this with Bobbie who suggested that I must have stolen it to purchase drugs.

For several months my mother had been making snide comments, telling me that she was going to find out what I was spending all of my money on because she knew that I was buying drugs with it. I never even responded to her accusations because I thought that what she was saying was totally absurd and I could not imagine where she came up with such ideas. She only had to look in my closet to discover what I had spent all of my money on – clothes. What I didn't know at the time was that it was Bobbie who had been stealing from my mother to buy drugs. Bobbie, it appears, was a drug addict as well as a prostitute. My mother sure did pick some nice friends.

Because I have always been incredibly forgetful with regard to my finances, I had been borrowing money from my sister to tide me over until the following pay day. Although I always paid Candice the money back, she has never been one to keep a secret, and must have said something to Mama about the fact that I borrowed money. With all these factors combined, Mama must have come to the conclusion that I was on drugs or something, stealing money to support my addiction.

One day when I was taking driving lessons at summer school, Bobbie, ever the instigator, waited for me outside of school and accosted me as I walked along the pavement with my friends. She grabbed me, forced me into the car, and drove me to my mother's beauty shop. I knew that my mother was upset about something, but I didn't know what. I decided to go outside and get some fresh air because it was quite obvious to me that I was not welcome in the shop. The moment I was outside, however, my mother swung open the door of the little trailer where she worked, and snarled, 'Where are you going?'

'I'm just going to get some fresh air,' I replied, quite confused as to why my mother was snapping at me so.

'I don't want you outside. I want you inside where I can keep an eye on you,' my mother snarled back.

As my mother stood in the centre of the small room, ratting a customer's hair, she made one sarcastic comment after another, directing them at me.

I had had enough of this because the plans that I had made for the day had been ruined. Since Bobbie had dragged me out of school, there was no way for me to get in touch with my friends and tell them what was going on. I was very upset, and asked my mother, 'What the hell is going on here?'

In front of her customers, Mama repeatedly pushed me against the wall, and I pushed her back.

At that, my mother told Bobbie to go out and get a switch to beat me with. Bobbie was all too happy to participate in child abuse, and soon reappeared with a limb from a tree. As my mother proceeded to hit me with it, it broke into pieces under the weight of her blows.

Still in the shop, in front of all her customers, she took the tree branch and flailed me with it, hitting me over and over. Something in me snapped, as my self-preservation mechanisms kicked in. For the only time in my life, I hit back. I took the tree branch out of my mother's hand and pushed her back, which left a small, red mark on her collarbone. Instantly, my mother and Bobbie were both on me. One of the two slammed me against the wall of the shop at full force. I really didn't want to fight with my mother, or Bobbie, or anybody. I just wanted them to stop hitting me.

When Bobbie saw that she had gotten the better of me, she started laughing in a gawky sort of way. My mother, however, became hysterical. How dare I push her! She had fogotten that it was she who struck the first blow. My mother had forgotten that she had sent Bobbie to my school to kidnap me, that she had taunted me in front of all of her customers, and that she had started beating me with a branch from a tree. Yet I, the errant child, was supposed to have had enough self-discipline not to defend myself when some crazy woman was attacking me.

Bobbie loved every minute of it. She hee-hawed in a silly, hillbilly sort of way, pointed to a dog that one of the customers had brought into the shop, and laughed, 'Even that dog could whip Krystal's ass.'

To this day, what truly amazes me is that my mother had such a demented attitude towards child-rearing that she felt that she had the right to attack me in front of a whole shop full of her customers. There is no way on this earth that I can understand why not one of her customers, who were looking on, intervene. Not one woman told my mother that she did not think it appropriate for her to be behaving such a way in a business establishment. Not one woman got up or told my mother that maybe it would be better if she could re-schedule her appointment for a time when it was more convenient for her to have clients. Not one person phoned the police and told them that there was a situation of domestic violence in the shop. Nothing. Not one step by any of those women to intervene. As far as I am aware, she did not lose any business whatsoever by her violent outburst.

After my mother and Bobbie had attacked me in full view of her clientele, I went into what can only be described as shock. My body had a mind of its own and I did not know what to do about it. Although I was conscious, I was shaking all over and felt tingles up and down my body. My mind could not believe it.

Having hurt me, my mother delighted in the anguish that she was causing me. She picked up her telephone, made me dial the number of my boss at work, and made me quit my job. My mother stood over me, grinning like a Cheshire cat, as I sobbed down the telephone line, trying to tell my boss that I was not allowed to go to work any more.

If all that were not bad enough, my mother, egged on by Bobbie, started threatening me. She said, 'I'm going to phone your father and have him come down here and beat you up. He broke my nose and he is going to break your nose too!' My mother assumed that my father would go over there and beat me up just because she wanted him to.

In another instant, she yelled at me, 'I'm going to have you put in Juvenile Hall! I'm going to have you put in a children's home!'

Since I was not allowed to go outside, I went into the bathroom and curled up in the foetal position on the floor. I just wanted everything to stop. I just wanted everything to go back to the way it had been.

But that was not the end of it. My mother next telephoned her mother, describing me dramatically as some sort of violent animal. My grandmother came over immediately and rushed into the bathroom where I was hiding, and proceeded to scream and yell at me as well.

'How could you do something like that?' she screeched. 'You might as well have done it to me! You might as well have done it to me!'

Finally, at about 6:00 or 7:00 that evening, I was told that we were going home. I dutifully piled into the back of the car with Mama and Bobbie up front. I just wanted to make things better and for the hell to end, and if it meant that I should apologise then that was what I would do. I told my mother that I was sorry.

I would admit defeat. I would take all of the blame. I did it all. It was all my fault. 'I'm sorry,' I said to my mother in a conciliatory voice.

'I know you are,' my mother replied, and I sensed a bit of weariness on her part.

I don't think that my mother had honestly thought it was going to go that far.

When we got home, Mama and Bobbie went into the house while Bill, my stepfather, stayed outside. I looked at Bill, and said, 'Do you know what they did to me?'

Mama had rung home to tell Bill all about it and I noticed too late that he was shaking with anger. 'I don't care what she did to you. I am concerned about what you did to your mother. I love her!'

Mama, in fact, couldn't stand the sight of him and was out on the town living it up absolutely every night of the week, but he 'loved' her. It was at that point that I knew that I did not have a friend in the world. I had thought that when we got home, Bill would get my mother to see reason. But when he made it clear to me that he thought that I was the culprit and did not think that my mother had done anything wrong, I knew that I was in really big trouble. With Bobbie egging my mother on, inciting her to commit even more atrocities, I could foresee that life would be hell from that day onward. I went to my room and stayed there.

After a while, my mother came to my bedroom and told me to take every stitch of clothing off. When I was completely naked, she told me to lie down on the bed and began beating me with a leather belt. Perhaps she learned to whip other naked women as one of the sex games that she played with her various girlfriends. Perhaps her parents did that sort of thing to her, which had the effect of warping her mind. Perhaps she just made it up as she went along, deriving more and more pleasure from every despicable act, becoming a dominatrix to an unwilling accomplice. Who knows where my mother learned to engage in such vulgarity, but the thought of what she did to me disgusts me. If my mother had not done such a depraved thing to me, I would never have imagined that a mother could do such a thing to her child.

My mother needed an audience to get the full feeling of satisfaction from her sadistic activities. She hadn't gleaned enough pleasure from making me undress and whipping me in the privacy of my own room. She made my sister come in.

I believe at that point that I must have lost consciousness and another personality took over my body to suffer the abuse, because my sister has had to fill me in on what followed. My sister has told me that for as long as she lives, she will never be able to get that horrible scene out of her head. My sister also told me that whenever she protested, my mother told her that she would get the same treatment if she dared to utter one word of reproach. Such was the inhumanity of the place that I once called home.

My mother then left the room and yelled for Candice to come downstairs. Candice was instructed to sit on the couch and watch. Mama then called for me. The personality who had taken over my body came into the living room wrapped in nothing but a blanket. Mama told me to put some clothes on and go into the den. The personality who had taken my body did as she was told. When the alternate personality went into the den, Mama instructed her to lie on the loveseat. The alternate personality put her head into the pillow as my mother beat my body on the legs and back until her arm hurt and she was tired.

Evidently, the cries were muffled in the pillow, but my sister was able to hear every whimper.

My mother beat my body and beat my body and beat my body. Finally, when she had worn herself out, she stopped.

'Mama, I love you, please stop,' the personality who had taken the beating whimpered to her tormentor. When my mother finally stopped beating the alternate personality who had taken over my body, she got up, went to my mother, and hugged her, and uttered the words, 'I love you.'

Well, I am here to tell you that from an early age I have not loved my mother! Even as young as the age of six or seven, when I was sitting at the dining hall at school, I knew I did not love her. Someone had given me a picture of my mother, who was considered to be very beautiful, to put in my little wallet. I looked at the picture of a supposedly attractive young woman, and all I could see was the ugly hag whom I hated! Even at that age, I knew not to tell people how I really felt about my mother. I took the picture and put it in my wallet without comment.

I have no idea who in the world it was who told my mother that she loved her, but it was not I!

The next thing that I remember after the beating was my mother sitting upstairs, cutting up some green beans that had been given to her. I thought that it was strange that she should be preparing green beans because she had never, ever, displayed the remotest interest in cooking, cleaning or anything that might be considered domestic.

Because my mother had telephoned everyone she could think of to tell them all kinds of stories about me, my grandmother and grandfather felt that they needed to come to the house. Because my mother was able to fabricate stories to make people feel sorry for her, they gave their condolences, believing every one of the lies that had crossed her lips.

The next morning at 5:00am, my mother kicked my bedroom door in. It was a Saturday and she told me to get out of bed and start cleaning the house. She also said that she was monitoring all of my phone calls, so I had better not try to phone anyone for help.

I got up and started cleaning. Bill did not speak to me because he was conspiring with my mother and Bobbie. He wanted to believe all of the things that Mama had told him. Candice did not dare speak to me because she had already been told that if she supported me, they would do the same thing to her that they had done to me. My brother was coming out of the hospital, but was in no position to do anything about it even if he wanted to.

The thought of leaving seemed totally alien to me because I did not have a place to stay, I did not have any money, and I could not even drive. I felt that I was bound to that place no matter what.

Even though I had been told not to use the telephone to make any outside phone calls, I picked it up and dialled the number at my paternal grandmother's house. When I told my grandmother what was going on she was horrified. She later told me that when I told her what they were doing, she spoke to Bill and informed him that if he laid one finger on me, she would phone the police and have him arrested. As far as I am concerned, the whole lot of them should have been put in jail.

That evening when my mother came home, the entire entourage was there to lend her support in what they imagined to be her hour of need. And of course, Bobbie was bustling around, spreading lies about me. To this day, I cannot understand how my mother allowed Bobbie to have such a huge influence over her, but she did.

The next day, which was a Sunday, was even more tense than before. As usual, all of my mother's family were gathered around. They didn't say a word to me, regarding me now as an evil person who had done all of these awful things; they were unwilling to hear anything that I had to say.

I don't know why, but I guess because no one else was speaking to me and I was so desperate, I spoke to Bobbie to feel her out. I have to hand it to Bobbie because she was able to play both sides of the fence with such ease. She could pretend to be my friend and stab me in the back at the same time. I had completely forgotten about that incident years before, when she had screamed at me that she was going to get me back for innocently telling my mother that she had gone to see one of her Johns.

That day I walked out in the woods and for the first time, I thought about ending my life to make all the pain go away. I had a kitchen knife with me and it would have been so easy to slit my wrists. In the end, however, I couldn't do it because as much as I wanted to die, I was equally terrified of blood.

I know that many people think that those who choose to end their lives are taking the coward's way out, and I do feel that sometimes it takes less strength to end one's life than to carry on living. But to make the conscious decision to terminate one's existence is acting decisively to change a bad situation – even if the outcome is on a more permanent basis. I do not regard myself as a strong person for not choosing to end my life on the many occasions since I was 16 when the pain inside of me was so great that I could scarcely bear to live any longer. What kept me alive was not that I wanted to stay and work my problems out, but rather an intense fear of the unknown. I honestly do not consider myself worthy of respect because I chose not to act on my first instinct, which was to end my life. The fact is that I was too much of a coward to take my own life when that is what I really wanted to do.

At the end of the day, I went back into that house because I did not know where else to go. But I had realised that my mother was never going to change and that I would be living in eternal Hell for as long as I stayed there. I told my mother that I wanted to go to my grandmother's house for the summer. In typical fashion, she replied, 'That's fine. You can go stay with your grandmother if you want. But, if you leave this house you can never come back.' Did she think that I would ever want to go back to that madhouse? I politely accepted my mother's ultimatum and started packing my bags. Although I had enough decorum not to say how I really felt, the fact was that once I got out of that house I had no intention of ever going back. To this day, what I find to be particularly odd is the fact that my mother apparently thought I would actually want to hang around and get abused all day long.

Everybody was happy that I was leaving. Mama was happy because she did not have to look after a child that she had never wanted anyway. Bill was happy because he never wanted any of my mother's children around anyway. Bobbie was happy because she wanted to do whatever it was she was doing with my mother unembarrassed by her children, who looked on with disapproval.

As I was packing my things to leave that house that had caused me so much anguish, my brother came and spoke to me. The only thing that Marc could find to say was, 'I think you're doing the right thing.'

Candice didn't say anything to me when I left because she was too frightened. Candice, if anything, is a survivalist and although she cared for me, she was not prepared to be treated the way I had been, and therefore chose to keep her mouth shut.

The only person to express any concern at all over the fact that I was leaving was my grandfather, who told me, 'I think you're making a big mistake.' I don't know why he said that. But of course, he did not know all of the things that his daughter had done to me. He did not have to live with her and be subjected, day in and day, out to her violent mood swings. But then again, from what I understand from my mother and her siblings, my grandfather was not averse to hitting his children if they got out of line, so I can only imagine that he didn't think my mother was doing anything wrong.

As I put all of my things in the car, Bill drove me to my grand-mother's house. I was happy to leave so that I could get some peace, and hoped that the Hell they had put me through would cease. Everyone else was happy for me to leave because they wanted to go back to their insane, dysfunctional lives and not have to worry that anyone might actually be concerned about the way that they were behaving.

When I left, I apparently wrote on a sheet of paper, 'The opposite of evil is live', and left the note for Candice. I very vaguely remember doing this. According to my sister, my mother took the note and read it out loud to her. The way my mother behaved frightened Candice so much that she has concluded that my mother must be possessed by demons. I have taken a less reli-gious view to analysing my mother's behaviour, however. I believe my mother has a severe personality disorder and should never, under any circumstances, be allowed near children or young people unsupervised.

My twin and I will be scarred from our mother's abuse for the rest of our lives. Even though the abuse I endured was targeted to harm me more extensively than my sister, in many ways I feel my sister has been more damaged. The things my mother did to me were so awful that I knew beyond a shadow of doubt that she was engaging in pure wickedness. The abuse my sister suffered, however, was much more subtle and left her wondering if it were all in her imagination. As a result of the abuse that my sister and I both endured, I have become a depressive, always wanting to take my life any time I become distraught. My twin, on the other hand, is more manic, always trying to find a suitable outlet for the anger and rage within her; an anger that she has never been able adequately to work through. My sister and I were, for want a better word, thrown away children.

While many people would be horrified that a woman would gain so much pleasure out of tormenting her daughter in such a humiliating fashion, apparently that practice is a perfectly acceptable way for many people to behave. In fact, such practices are endorsed by the United States armed forces.

On 28th April 2003 the *Daily Mirror* printed the article entitled, 'Naked Agression', which is related as follows:

> 'Stripped at gunpoint and publicly branded as thieves a gang of suspected Iraqi looters are humiliated by US troppers' street justice. 'After being hauled before a kangaroo court, the men had the words of Ali Baba Haram-Arabic for '...dirty thief, he stole's... crawled on their chests with a marker pen. 'They were paraded in front of a jeering Baghdad crowd before fleeing to safety'.
>
> 'The '...appalling...' affront to dignity outraged human rights organizations who say it broke the Geneva

Convention, which protects prisoners against '...insults or public curiosity...'. 'It fuelled Iraqi resentment at the US '...occupation...'of their country, provoked dozens of demonstrations and flew in the face of guidelines aimed at winning over the locals.

'But the trooper allegedly responsible was defiant. First Lieutenant Eric Canady of Delta Squadron's 10th Engineer Corps said '...I don't think this kind of action is excessive. We've done it once before to another man we found looting and it worked perfectly...'

'Raw justice was handed down when the US soldiers arrested four men in Baghdad's Zawra Amusement Park on suspicion of looting. 'After questioning and searching the suspects – and with the prison system in chaos – the troopers were at a loss to know where to take them. 'So they made their own brutal law. Lieutenant Canady allegedly asked a group of watching Iraqis how the men should be punished. 'Troops said they were told the best way would be to brand them thieves and strip them.

'The fearful suspects were shoved at gunpoint into a tent where they were stripped. 'With the help of a Muslim soldier in the unit they were in they daubed with insults and forced into the streets to brave a crowd screaming '...Ali Baba..!' One of the men, Zian Djumma, 20, said later, '...It was horrendous. Now I want to find a hand grenade and throw it at the soldiers. I hate them for this...'

'He said he and his friends had entered the park, used by Saddam Hussein's Republican Guard for weapons storage, to search for one of their men's young brothers. 'Troops said the men were carrying a bag of parts for weapons.

'Coming on top of an explosion at the US arms dump in the city, which killed up to 40 Iraqis and seriously injured 60, the degrading scenes brought an explosion of fury.

'Demonstrating outside the city's Palestine Hotel, Adil Al-Harni, 41, said last night: '...This is a disgusting way to treat people without trying them. How do we know these men are thieves? Even if they were, this is no way to treat them. If this is US democracy, they can keep it. It's just another way of keeping people in their place. I believe it will cause big trouble...'

'Amnesty International said, '...It was an appalling way to treat prisoners. Such degrading treatment is a clear violation of US responsibilities. The US authorities must investigate this incident and publicly release the findings...'

'The Red Cross added: '...The Americans have a responsibility to give good treatment to all prisoners, whoever they are...'

'US Central Command have pledged a probe. '...The '...Ali Baba...' row is the latest in a string of embarrassing incidents for the US Military in which troops have flouted guidelines on how to win Iraqis, '...hearts and minds...'

'US troops have raised the Stars and Stripes at captured sites on several occasions. Most notoriously on a statue of Saddam during the last push into Baghdad. 'But allied forces were specifically ordered against such displays as it was believed the population would feel humiliated by the sight of the foreign flag flying in the homeland.'

One question that needs to be asked is where did human beings learn to treat other human beings so inhumanely? When exactly did society become numb to the many injustices of the world. I don't think that it would be unreasonable to assume that those soldiers who humiliated the looters had been humiliated themselves at some point because if they had been raised in a loving manner it would be highly unlikely that they would be capable of such an abuse of power. People are taught by example, so if a young person witnesses violence and degradation then he will come to believe that such behaviour is acceptable.

Many people believe charity begins in the home. In the same line of thinking, it can also be said that cruelty begins in the home as well.

Air Force Blues

27th March 1979 was a pivotal day in my life. It was the day I left Little Rock, never to return for anything more than a few days every several years or so. At the time of this writing I have not been back for more than ten years.

I knew I was making a mistake. I secretly felt the military was beneath me, but I allowed a friend to talk me into enlisting one day when I was feeling blue. The route to my joining the Air Force was rather strange. I was with a group of friends who decided they wanted to eat a meal at Casa Bonita, a Mexican restaurant, and not pay for it. I tried to convince Sherry, my errant friend, not to do it, but she would not listen to common sense. As a result, the police were called and my friend was arrested.

Because Sherry was not yet 18, she had to spend the night in Juvenile Hall. During her stay, she was required to speak to a counsellor and during the counselling session it was decided that she should join the military.

Personally, I think those counsellors who speak to troubled young people quite often do more harm than good. I believe they are told they have to plant the idea of joining the military into the minds of these young, impressionable people as a short-term measure. Encouraging young people who have behavioural problems to join the military gets them out of the jurisdiction. I do not think that Sherry really seriously wanted to join the military, but her counsellor suggested it to her. Being quite disturbed through her various life experiences, Sherry was led to feel that joining the military would answer all of her problems. I believe the counsellor who spoke to Sherry was instructed to plant the idea of joining the military into the minds of all young people he met, thereby putting the problem of dealing with a disturbed person who had been neglected, abused and traumatised into the hands of another agency far away from Arkansas. Sadly, those counsellors are not solving problems, but merely exporting them.

I suppose the authorities believe that they are doing what is best by encouraging young people from dysfunctional backgrounds to join the armed forces. It is true that the military affords young people a much better life than many of them have had with their own parents and guardians. Life may be bad in the military, but it was much worse at home.

In my case I did not have a home or any family who gave a damn enough to care what I did. Although I phoned my mother and told her that I was leaving to join the Air Force, she could not be bothered to see me off. Now, if it had been one of her girlfriends leaving, she would have made the time to say goodbye: that is something that I know for a fact. Sherry did not want to join the Air Force on her own, so she pestered me relentlessly until I gave in. I really didn't want to join the military, but I went along with her to the recruiting station to speak to the recruiter. Personally, I thought it was all a big joke, but went ahead and answered all of the questions to the best of my ability. At the end of the interview, we were all weighed and I was told that at 141 pounds, I was three pounds overweight and therefore not eligible for military service. I really didn't want to join the Air Force anyway, so was not upset in the least to learn that I was overweight.

The strange thing is that I suddenly lost my appetite. In the span of a month, I had lost seven pounds and was therefore within the acceptable weight range to join the armed forces, if that was what I wanted to do. Destiny has a funny way of working because, in addition to losing my appetite, I was also in the process of letting go of personal relationships that might have kept me in Little Rock. I had been dating a local rogue and he promptly dumped me and abandoned me on the outskirts of town when he found out that I would not go to bed with him. This man was definitely not a gentleman!

With no decent accommodation, no job worth having and no boyfriend, there was not much keeping me in Little Rock. Therefore, on the spur of the moment, I decided to trade in my pathetic existence in Arkansas for an adventure that would take me to different states, countries and even continents. If I had never joined the United States Air Force, I may never have left Little Rock.

While the military has many good points, it also has downsides. It is a disciplined, regimented organisation. Because such a career is so taxing on the body, mind and soul, it would seem reasonable to assume that they would recruit only the smartest and best elements of society, but instead the opposite is quite often the case.

Instead of recruiting people who have stable backgrounds and good standards of education, they look for those individuals whom society has overlooked, those persons with no qualifications, a dysfunctional family background, and no stability. Because the military tends to recruit from socially and economically deprived backgrounds, is it any wonder that there are so many problems with bullying, harassment and abuse within the profession. The recruitment policy has created an excellent breeding ground for disaster.

The *News of the World* published the following article on 28th July 2002:

> 'Four soldiers based at America's top Special Forces barracks have murdered their wives in a month. 'Three of the men had just returned from dangerous duty in Afghanistan. 'All of the soldiers were based at Fort Bragg,

North Carolina – home to elite troops who are the equivalent of our own SAS.

'The American Special Forces tough training regime is famed for teaching troopers to kill instinctively and without compunction in hand to hand combat.

'The first wife to die was Teresa Nieves. Her husband, Sgt 1st Class Rigoberto Nieves, shot her at their home on 11th June. 'He then shot himself. Nieves had been home from Afghanistan for just two days on leave to resolve personal problems.

In the second murder, Master Sgt William Wright strangled his wife, Jennifer. Her mother, Wilma, said Wright, who had been back from Afghanistan for only a month, was 'getting attacks of rage'.

'Third to die was Marilyn Griffin. Her estranged husband, engineer Sgt Cedric Ramon Griffin, is charged with stabbing her 50 times.

Sgt 1st Class Brandon Floyd made his wife the fourth victim, shooting her and then himself. 'Floyd was in the ultra-secret anti-terrorist Delta Force and had been home from Afghanistan since January. 'Andrea's mother, Penny, said: 'I believe his training was such that if you can't control it, you kill it.'

'The murders were the first at Fort Bragg for two years.

'Garrison chief Col. Tad Davis was 'surprised and saddened' by the killings and pledged an urgent review of procedures.'

Something must be terribly wrong with a profession that teaches its members to be misogynistic, wife-beating murderers, but that is exactly the philosophy the armed forces instils in its serving members.

The military brainwashes servicemen into believing that having a spouse and a family is not compatible with serving their country, and as a result they soon treat their wives and children with the same degree of disrespect and disregard they must endure in their profession. Is it any wonder, therefore, that military children are the worst behaved children in the world and military wives are often unkempt and shabbily dressed, with no respect for themselves or their bodies.

The famous military brainwashing slogan goes something like, 'If the Army (or Air Force, Navy or Marines) wanted you to have a wife (or family) they would have issued you one.' I must have heard that saying a thousand times. Unfortunately, if people tell you something long enough, you will actually start to believe it. Service members are made to feel guilty for wanting a family, so it is not surprising that they treat their partners and children so badly.

Don't be fooled, America is just as good at propaganda as their enemy countries. If anything, America is better at it. How else could the American establishment get grown men and women to forsake their families and their own personal destinies for causes that they do not really believe in if they were not good at propaganda, manipulation and brainwashing?

Because people in the armed forces must often carry weapons and are expected to lay down their lives for their country, it would be reasonable to expect servicemen to have a fair amount of control. Unfortunately, the opposite is often the case. A damaged individual from an unstable background must be able to work through his own past traumas and put them into perspective before he can reasonably be expected to exercise self-control. The fact is, however, that while in the military, he is often thrown into a very stressful 24-hour-a-day vocation with no time to rest his soul and reflect on his and others' lives. As a result, many military members are living on borrowed time, waiting for that one crucial moment when they will lose control and do something they will later regret.

The following article appeared in the 22nd August, 2002 issue of the *Daily Mail*:

'A British soldier serving in Afghanistan shot his sergeant eight times as he relaxed in a hammock and then turned the gun on himself. 'It was reported that Sergeant Robert Busuttil and Corporal John Gregory, both 30, had been drinking at a farewell barbecue at a small British military base near Kabul airport when they died.

'The Defence Ministry did not say how the two soldiers, both members of the Royal Logistics Corps, were killed. 'But yesterday Sergeant Busuttil's father released his version of the incident after speaking to an officer on peacekeeping duties in Kabul.

'A family statement said the pair had argued on Friday night and that Corporal Gregory from North Yorkshire shot sergeant Busuttil, from Swansea, before killing himself.

'During the evening, banter took place between Sergeant Busuttil and Corporal Gregory,' the statement said. At some stage, Sergeant Busuttil made a comment and Corporal Gregory swung a punch. Sergeant Busuttil retaliated and punched Corporal Gregory twice, at which point the altercation was halted. 'The two men then sat and talked and had a drink together – as far as everyone was aware, the issue was resolved.

'When the function drew to a close most people, including Corporal Gregory, left. Some 40 minutes later, Sergeant Busuttil was outside in a hammock, chatting with two fellow soldiers, when Corporal Gregory approached.

'The family said Corporal Gregory then fired five rifle rounds into Sergeant Busuttil's stomach and, as he slumped forward, a further three rounds into his back. Corporal Gregory then aimed the gun under his chin and fired the weapon, killing himself.

'The family said this version of events had been told to them by a British officer, with the permission of the Ministry of Defence.

'...We could have eventually accepted, however sad and difficult it would have been, if Bob had died in military action, but to think he was killed by one of his own fellow soldiers is incomprehensible.

'...Right now, all of our thoughts are focused on bringing Bob home to Swansea and ensuring he receives a dignified funeral. We hope the formal investigation into the awful event is carried out swiftly.'

'The two soldiers were part of a small British contingent in the Internal Security Assistance Force. 'The commanding officer of British forces in Kabul said a police investigation is underway and a coroner's court will be convened in England. The MoD refused to comment. 'The deaths bring the total number of fatalities involving British troops in Afghanistan to three.'

The above article clearly illustrates that rather than having self control, service members quite often lack it. They live their lives to excess in many ways, such as smoking, drinking and sexual promiscuity. On some military installations, such as in the Far East, airmen and soldiers are actually given condoms when they leave the front gate. Although those condoms are meant as a safety measure to protect against highly dangerous venereal diseases, such as the 'black syph' (a highly dangerous form of syphilis), they are nonetheless sending the wrong message to young men. The message is, 'Sleep with as many women as you like, just make sure you protect yourself.'

The military also creates a lot of bullies who thrive on threats and intimidation. In fact, the prospect of dominating others is one of the things that attracts many damaged souls to the profession.

On 28th July 2002, the *News of the World* published an exposé of Deepcut Barracks, a British Army training installation. The goings-on at Deepcut have sparked intense media attention, so much so that in November 2002 it was revealed that the military installation is to be closed down altogether because the stigma surrounding serious allegations of misconduct by officers in that camp was regarded as ineradicable. If Deepcut Barracks were closed, speculation into what really went on at that installation would die down. Well, that is the plan anyway.

Although the article concerned the British Army, it is highly unlikely that the Americans would have behaved any differently. This exposé should be seen, therefore, as a reflection of the military institution as a whole, and blame should not be placed on one particular culture or nation.

'Police have reopened enquiries into the deaths of four privates who all died from gunshot wounds. Originally the Ministry of Defence ruled that all deaths were suicide.

'The *News of the World* investigated the situation and found that the Army had destroyed key documents within hours of one of the deaths. They even got rid of one man's kit.

'Since 1995, when the first 'suicide' took place, there have been 28 court-martials for violent conduct at the base.

'Bullying goes on in most camps,' said a retired major, who spoke to the *News of the World* on the condition that his identity was protected. 'Most units try to stop it, but not at Deepcut. It was physical, mental and intimidating. They would get a guy on a table, strip him to the waist, hold a red hot iron half an inch from his chest so he could feel the heat. When he was trembling with fear, his eyes closed in terror, they'd slap an ice cold mess tin on him instead. The first sensation of extreme cold is much like extreme heat. Obviously the victim thought it was the iron and was terror struck. His tormentors thought it was great fun. I tried hard to stamp it out.'

'Warrant Officer Michael Nation, who ran the Sergeants' Mess for seven years until January 2002, told the *News of the World* he was appalled with the mess when he took it over.

'It was like a brothel. There were 90 rooms and everyone seemed to be at it. When I'd arrive in the morning, I'd see women dashing out of NCOs' flats and going off to work. In many cases, they never came out of the same flat twice. In my naivety, when I first saw female recruits streaming to the flats at the back of the mess, I thought they were going to do fatigues for officers like cleaning, washing and ironing. I soon learned. These guys were regulars at a local night-club called Joe Bananas. They'd march on to the parade square, pick out female recruits they fancied, then find some fault – anything would do. Then the recruit would be told something like, "I won't put you on charge now. Just make sure you're at Joe Bananas tonight." I became friendly with women sergeants who knew how to look after themselves but even they were frightened of the bullying. Even young male officers were demanding sex from the female recruits. It was going all over the place. I remember on one occasion – it was a very hot day – when an officer and his cronies were making the unit patrol around the parade ground. The unit was in heavy No.2 uniform and they were melting. But the officer and his pals watched with their shirt sleeves rolled up – and they were sipping port! They were always picking on the waitresses. One sergeant major always made them take his breakfast on a tray to his flat and sometimes made them give him his breakfast in bed, which raised more than a few eyebrows. We had to put a stop to that and told the girls to leave the tray outside his door. But I also remember once the same officer made a girl go to his flat and cut his toenails!'

'The first of the four soldiers to die was 20-year-old Private Sean Benton, from Hastings, East Sussex. In July 1995 he was found dead with five gunshot wounds to the chest, apparently fired from a long range. The initial Army finding was suicide.

'This was confirmed by a coroner but Benton's mother, Linda, believes he was shot by someone else. Former soldier Trevor Hunter, who was at the base with Sean, said his friend was beaten up and even thrown out of a second floor window by Deepcut bullies.

'Mr Hunter, who quit the Army 2 years ago after 6 years service, told how just a day before this apparent suicide, Pte Benton was singled out because he said he didn't like football. He was made to pray in front of a jerry can painted in Newcastle United colours and told to ask 'Private Jerry Can' for forgiveness.

'I'd took Sean under my wing because I could see people were picking on him,' said Mr Hunter. 'He was an easy target because he had a creaky voice, he spoke his mind, and his kit was a mess.'

'In November 1995, the body of Pte Cheryl James, 18, was found in the woodland just outside the Deepcut perimeter fence. Her rifle was by her side. Initial Army finding: suicide. But this time, an inquest did not agree. A coroner recorded an open verdict.

'Last September, Pte Geoff Gray, just 17, was found dead with gunshot wounds above each eye. Initial Army finding: suicide. But a coroner ruled emphatically that he did not think the private took his own life.

'Pte Gray's father talked to a forensic expert who examined photographs of his son's body.

'He said it was unlikely that Geoff could get into that position and get one bullet into his head, let alone two. The spread of powder burns on his face was desperately unusual.' It also emerged that all of Pte Gray's clothes had been destroyed after his death. So were log books recording the serial number of the SA80 rifle he was using.

'Mr Gray commented, 'It means the police don't know whether the gun which killed my son was his or not.'

'An army spokesman said the disposal of items was routine procedure after initial enquiries into a death were completed.

'In March 2002, Pte James Collinson, also 17, died from a single gunshot wound to the head. Initial Army finding: suicide. His father, Jim Collinson, insisted, 'The Army have tried to sweep this whole affair under the carpet and seem to believe they have no one to answer to. It's disgraceful.'

'According to insiders at the camp there has been fresh scandal in the past few weeks. A private is said to have taken an overdose and a corporal was caught having sex with a young female soldier. 'The MoD has confirmed that an 'inappropriate' relationship between a corporal and a private took place and said an internal investigation was taking place.'

After having read the above news clips, which were all written within a brief period of time, it seems evident that something is terribly wrong in the military establishment. The military recruits are individuals from economically and socially deprived areas who bring their morals and values with them. Those who were once victims become victimisers. Those who were once abused become abusers. Those who were once bullied become bullies.

Child abuse and the military establishment have closely defined links because only a person who has been harmed can contemplate harming another. Sadly, the military is often the perfect vehicle that will allow damaged, wounded souls to express the deeply repressed, unresolved rage they feel about the injustices done to them as children.

Alice Miller is a psychoanalyst who has worked extensively on the causes and effects of child abuse; on violence towards children and its cost to society. She has analysed the lives of many figures in German history, including Adolf Hitler and Fredrich Nietzsche. In her work, *The Untouched Key*, she offers some insights that aptly reflect the mind of a battered child. Alice Miller has noted that every aggressive reaction on the child's part to abuse is suppressed, and the suppression laid the foundation for destructive behaviour in adulthood. And yet there must always have been individual parents who were capable of giving love and who provided their children with a counter-balance for the cruelty they suffered. Above all, however, there must have been helping witnesses present in the person of nannies, household staff, aunts, uncles, siblings, or grandparents who did not feel responsible for raising the child and who were not camouflaging cruelty as love because they had experienced love in their own childhoods. If this were not the case, the human race would have died long ago. On the other hand, if there had been more mothers and fathers capable of love, our world would be different today; it would be more humane. People would also have a clear understanding of what love is because they would have experienced it in childhood and it would be unconceivable for biographers to call something an expression of material love that in its essence was a prison, concentration camp, or brainwashing institute. Yet, according to most of today's biographers, Stalin and Hitler had 'loving mothers'. It seems inconceivable that the world at large is being led to believe that two of the biggest murderers in the history of mankind had 'loving mothers'. Surely, if they did indeed have loving mothers, they would not have been compelled to commit all of the atrocities they did.

When punishment is held up as proof of love, children are filled with confusion, which bears bitter fruit later in life. If these children become involved in politics, they continue the work of destruction initiated on them in childhood, and they camouflage it by taking on the role of saviour, just as their parents before them. Both Stalin and Hitler claimed that they only wanted to do well. This ideology was passed on to them by both parents. If this had not been so, if one parent had served as a helping witness and shielded the child from the other parent's brutality and coldness, the children would not have become criminals in later life.

Thus, politicians can profess to be peace-loving Christians and at the same time advocate the production of weapons 5 million times more powerful than the Hiroshima bomb. These politicians can defend without a qualm the necessity for an absurd arms race because they learned long ago not to feel. It is therefore possible for those caught in this kind of mental system to plan multiple Hiroshima catastrophes and still to pray in church every Sunday for peace; what is more, they consider themselves entitled to bear the responsibility for the fate of the whole world because they are advanced in years, because they have experience in wars.

Like children who endure psychic death to preserve the illusion of having an intelligent, foresightful father, soldiers go to war to die for the leader who misuses them. That has been the way of the world.

So there you have it. A battered child from a highly dysfunctional family entered into an equally dysfunctional profession. I had never been given a chance to heal the wounds caused by my childhood traumas before I went into an equally destructive job.

I completed my basic training at Lackland Air Force Base, Texas. It was there that I was indoctrinated into the many mind games that military leaders play on their soldiers, sailors and airmen to get them to toe the party line.

Our training instructors, or TIs, would make us get up at 5:00am each day for compulsory exercise and running around a track. By the end of our six-week basic training, we would be required to run a mile and a half in less than 15 minutes. Our day was filled with lessons and exams to prepare us for life in the military institution.

I was an easy person to brainwash because I had come from such a dysfunctional family and had already experienced many traumatic events. Through years of abuse and neglect, I had learned that any attention was better than no attention at all. The military had become my family. It had replaced my biological family, who never really wanted me anyway.

I remember with clarity how our TIs would yell at us for any real or imagined wrong. One day, a young recruit had had enough of her TI barking commands at her. At the top of her lungs, she retaliated with a scream of 'Fuck you!', to a rather astonished group of people in the centre of the dining facility, commonly called a chow hall. After the irate recruit had said her piece, she stormed out of the chow hall, to the amazement of everyone who heard it. I remember being totally aghast that the young recruit would say such a thing. I would never have declared my feelings to one of the TIs, whom I saw as almost on a par with God himself.

Although the young woman could have made her feelings known in a more educated and tactful manner, the point was that she thought enough of herself not to tolerate another person's verbally abusing her, no matter who that person might be. She did not see the TIs as superior beings, but as what they actually were, bullies.

It should come as no surprise to learn that, aside from the fact that the military is not a suitable environment for anyone who is an independent thinker, the services actually do not want people who will stand up for themselves, speak their mind and can think for themselves. Therefore, within minutes, the errant recruit was located and promptly processed for discharge.

It was also in basic training that I experienced my own share of bullying and harassment. I was an easy person to pick on because I have a strong southern accent and, because of my rather austere upbringing, I lacked valuable social skills to be able to mix with a crowd of people.

The TIs would get on me about my marching technique, my hair, and just about anything else they could think of. Even though I was harassed by the TI on a daily basis, surprisingly I did not get one AF Form 341, which was a document recruits had to carry in their pocket and hand to a TI for any real or imagined wrong that they had committed. The fact that I was not required to give my TI a 341 is clear evidence that I could not have been that bad a recruit.

Although I may not appear to be all there, am not terribly coordinated, and do not possess many of the social skills necessary to be a real success in life, I nevertheless have a will as strong as iron. So many times in my childhood, I should have died; I was starved, beaten and disfigured by those people who professed to care, but I lived through it all. Damaged though I was, I was still alive. Therefore, even though I was not pleased about the fact that I had been targeted for bullying, I weathered the storm and graduated from basic training along with the rest of my flight. I would also like to point out that my TI later told me that he did not think that I would finish basic training. How little that man knew about me.

There was one incident that happened during basic training that I did not quite understand at the time. A woman in my flight who had a husband and two small children living in the base airmen's quarters, or BAQ, had the horror of having her four-year-old daughter abducted.

This woman's child literally vanished into thin air. I had blocked my own experiences of childhood sexual abuse, so I could not understand how a child could just disappear. The fact that someone would take the child was a totally alien concept to me. At that time, I did not know that virtually all children who are abducted are murdered by their abductors within three days.

Sadly, my TIs lost interest in harassing me and began instead picking on this poor woman for any real or imagined wrong. They criticised her for her marching technique and I could not help wondering if they were being a bit harsh on her, especially considering the fact that she had just lost her child. But that is the whole nature of bullying. A bully would never dream of picking on someone who can fight back because, underneath his bravado, he is in fact a coward.

One incident that stands out in my mind was one morning when a group of ladies and myself were called into an office to speak to our TI. We were lined up in a row and made to stand at attention while our TI bawled us out because we were less than ten pounds under our maximum allowable weight, mine being 138 pounds.

All at once the absurdity of the situation I found myself in overtook me. Who cared if I were a few pounds overweight? In the grand scheme of things, did it really matter? Even though I was standing at attention listening to my TI rant on about my weight, I could not stop myself from laughing. I tried as hard as I could to keep my composure and appear serious, but it was just too much. I thought for sure that I would be singled out and yelled at some more, but surprisingly, I wasn't. I suppose even my TI knew that the Air Force was being a bit petty about the weight issue.

It is not as if I had not heard it all before. From the time I was in grade school, my mother and father made a big deal about how much I weighed. Because they both were constantly picking on me about how much I should weigh, they sent the message across to my brother and cousins that it was okay to harass me about my weight.

My brother, cousins and father made fun of me, called me names, and generally made my life a misery. To be honest, by today's standards I was actually quite petite, but to hear them talk one would have thought I was a beached whale.

Much to the surprise of my TI, I finished basic training and was sent to Keesler Air Force Base, Mississippi, to attend a technical training school to become a radio relay equipment repairman.

After 17 weeks of training, I was sent to Andrews Air Force Base, Maryland, to work in the Electronic Maintenance section. When I arrived in Maryland, I was taken to the barracks, where I had been assigned a room that I would be required to share with another woman whom I had never met.

It is funny, really, to think that I gave up so many of my rights and my own self-determination. I was told where I would live, where I would work, and what I would do both at work and in my free time. I had allowed myself to be told what do to for such a large extent of my life that slowly but surely I was losing the ability to determine my own destiny. It was such a gradual process that I never even realised what was happening to me.

Before I knew it, the United States Air Force had got me. They owned me, body, mind and soul.

Enrique

It was in the Electronic Maintenance work centre that I was to meet Enrique, an individual who would have such a profound impact on my life. Enrique was 5'8" tall, brown-skinned with curly black hair and penetrating black eyes. I had never met a Puerto Rican before and I found him to be a totally exotic person.

In Arkansas, one was either black or white, and interracial marriages were still considered taboo. Enrique, however, was neither black nor white, being a mixture of of both. He had the hair, eyes and a few physical characteristics of a black person, but he also resembled a white person. He was one person who could not be pigeon-holed into one specific race. I never considered Enrique to be one race or another. All I knew was that he was someone whom I definitely wanted to be a part of my life.

Although Enrique had his fair share of problems, in many ways he was more advantaged than I was. He already had an electronics background when he joined the Air Force, having studied it in college, and therefore had an advantage over his contemporaries. More importantly, he came from a relatively decent family who ensured he was adequately fed, clothed, loved and well educated. Enrique had finished first in his high school class, then went on to college on a scholarship. I find it quite unbelievable that a man who had the advantage of a high IQ and a supportive family could turn out to be such an underachiever, but I suppose anything is possible in this strange world we live in.

Being a battered, neglected and rejected child, I never had the benefit of a good standard of education. I had to quit school at 16 and was awarded a General Education Diploma, or GED, when I was 17. Because I was so young and naïve, I did not pick up on Enrique's dark side, as a more streetwise individual might have done. Although Enrique was intelligent enough to be able to go to college on a scholarship, he failed to complete his academic work. It was at college that Enrique must have undergone a personality change because he stopped doing his assignments and eventually dropped out altogether. So profound was this personality change that one of his lecturers actually felt the need to speak to him about his obvious lack of performance.

Enrique's father had stopped working years before, which certainly did not present a good role model for his family. Enrique's mother went to work every day in a factory and his father slept in, met up with his other unemployed friends to play dominos and ran a numbers racket based on the Puerto Rican lottery. Because the Latin American culture dictates that the woman is expected to pander to the man's every whim, Enrique's father did not feel the need to left a finger around the house either. As a consequence, he contributed absolutely nothing to the household, which certainly put a deep strain on the marriage. The troubled marriage no doubt left deep scars on Enrique's psyche, leaving him with a very dark personality, which few people would be aware of. Such a difficult home life would go on to form Enrique's patterns of thought, ensuring that he would go on to treat me in the same way that his father treated his mother, if not worse.

Enrique's family situation was rather unusual, but it was a definite improvement over mine. His parents moved to America so their children could get a good education, and for the sake of the children, they at least tried to be civil to each other even though they had stopped sharing a bed years earlier.

The big difference between Enrique's family and mine was that, as imperfect as they were, they actually cared about their children and had a strong support network of family and friends.

I had none of that. If I had, perhaps I would have been inclined towards healthier, more fulfilling interpersonal relationships. If I had had the benefit of a decent family then I might not have been attracted to someone like Enrique in the first place.

Enrique's family was not happy at all about the fact he had joined the Air Force. I suspect he did it in an attempt to exert his independence because he told me that he hated his father's trying to control him. It is funny, really, how history tends to repeat itself, because Enrique would attempt to control others in the same fashion that his father attempted to control him.

From what I understand, Enrique dropped out of college and was drifting aimlessly through life. He had become a major underachiever by the time he was only 21. At least the Air Force gave him a sense of purpose, which is something that he would never garner in his home town of Lawrence, Massachusetts.

I was totally enamoured with the fact that Enrique had a college education. I had quit school at 16 and never in a million years did I imagine that I would be able to attend college. I thought that because Enrique had a college education, he had the potential to make something of his life. I thought he was really special. Oh, how wrong I was.

Enrique had been nicknamed the Love Machine by a group of friends he hung out with. I thought he had been given the nickname because he was a real heart throb with the ladies, but I would later discover that I had been the only woman whom he had ever been intimate with. When I first laid eyes on Enrique, I was quite intrigued and made it my business to get to know him. I spent a great deal of time talking to him at his workstation and took every opportunity to speak to him during the day. I even quit smoking because I thought he would like me more if I were a non-smoker.

Enrique seemed quite fond of me but at the same time appeared ambivalent about dating me. This became clear to me when I went to his workstation to say hello and he chastised me, telling me that I should not be speaking to him at work. My feelings were quite hurt that he should say such a thing to me. I nevertheless buried the hurt feelings and carried on with my duties, determined that I would not bother with him any more. I very much wish that I had carried on with my resolve to forget all about Enrique because I should have been spared decades of heartache if I had. Enrique, it seemed, preferred the company of men. There were two men he worked with whom he did practically everything with. If he wanted to be with them more than with me, then I would just leave him to it.

But it wasn't as simple as that. Enrique was sending me very mixed messages. He would not ask me out on a proper date, but at the same time he would make eye contact with me. At one time he even stared at me intently while he brushed my finger against his when we were amongst a group of people at work. One evening Enrique rang me and asked me if I would like to go out with him but I could not go because I had already made plans. I was very disappointed and was worried that I had missed my big chance. Finally, he asked me go to a Halloween party with him at the non-commissioned officers, or NCO, Club, and I accepted. The sexual chemistry between us was so intense that I could not keep my hands off him. At one point during the evening, someone we worked with told us that we would have to tone down our behaviour, but I didn't care. I was so attracted to Enrique that I did not even notice what was going on around me.

When we left the party, we drove to a secluded place and we 'parked'. We made out in the back seat of the car and years later I learned that I was the first woman Enrique had ever been with. I was quite surprised about this because in Arkansas everyone was experiencing carnal knowledge at a very young age, perhaps for no other reason than they were bored and had nothing better to do.

As fate would have it, while we were being intimate with one another, a security policeman tapped on the window and told us that we should not be parking there, thus putting an end to our evening of passion.

Shortly after our date, Enrique decided to take a week's leave and visit his family in Lawrence. He had not made any other plans to see me, so I just assumed that I liked him more than he liked me and should therefore not get my hopes up. I was surprised, however, when he phoned me while he was on leave.

While Enrique was on leave, I carried on with work as normal. One evening Carlos, one of my colleagues, gave me a lift home. While I sat in his car, he told me that he did not get along with Enrique. Carlos told me that in the summer, they were playing softball for the 2045th Communication Group's softball team and he and Enrique had got into a dispute whilst playing the game. Carlos told Enrique that if he wanted to settle the dispute, they could take their disagreement elsewhere and indicated that he would quite happily get into a fist fight if that were what it took. When Enrique saw that Carlos meant business and was not afraid to fight, he backed down. From that point forward, Carlos had little, if any, respect for Enrique.

At that time I really didn't understand the full implication of what Carlos had told me. What I would realise later was that while Enrique would back down from a fight if he thought he might get hurt, he did not mind picking on people smaller or weaker than himself. Therefore, while he would never dream of picking on someone his own size or someone whom he thought might fight back, he considered women, and possibly even children, fair game. I did not know it at the time, but Enrique was a bully. Like virtually all bullies, he would only pick on those who he thought would not or could not fight back.

It was also while Enrique was on leave that he was given an assignment to Turkey. One of the major disadvantages of being a radio relay equipment repairman was that our career field had to go on a lot of remote tours. Enrique was devastated when he was given the assignment, which was a 12-month remote tour. He tried everything he could think of to get out of it, but nothing seemed to work.

Finally, he decided that he would to speak to the base chaplin. I had no idea why he felt the need to speak to the chaplin, but I kept my concerns to myself, not even asking what he was going to say to the man. Whatever Enrique did say to the chaplin did not have the desired effect, however, because he was still going to Turkey whether he liked it or not.

It was also when he was given the posting to Turkey that Enrique's attitude towards me changed. While he had previously been ambivalent towards me and was not particularly bothered about how much time he spent with me, he now had a complete change of heart and saw me every day after he received the news.

I found sex with Enrique quite difficult because he was very well endowed and his sexual organs were just too large for my comparatively small frame. He also had a problem in that he could not have a climax, which made sex with me even more painful. On one occasion, I was so badly damaged that I could barely walk for a week. I was in excruciating pain because all of my sexual organs had been rubbed raw!

I made the dire mistake of telling Enrique about my sexual history, which was really quite tame by today's standards. He, however, seemed to think that I was a slut because I was not a virgin when we met, and he treated me accordingly. I had such a low opinion of myself that it never occurred to me to expect to be treated with a little respect and courtesy from my boyfriend.

On another occasion, Enrique was visiting me in my room. We were both lying on my bed, relaxing, talking about nothing in particular. Out of the blue, he said that I would sleep with just about anybody. I was totally taken aback that he could say such a thing to me. I was supposed to be his girlfriend and I felt that I was deserving of a bit more respect than that. Besides, what he said was not true. I have had hundreds of invitations for sex and have declined the vast majority of them.

I was so hurt by what Enrique had said that I needed to be on my own and asked him to leave. He was surprised that I asked him to go. He did not expect me, or any woman for that matter, to exert her independence. Sadly, that was one of the few times in my life when I ever did anything to prove my own worth to myself.

That evening, I went to work on a mid-shift, which was from 12:00 midnight until 8:00 in the morning. I did not give my relationship with Enrique much thought that evening. I did not consider our relationship to be serious at that time, so it would have been very easy for me to walk away from a man who I would later discover to be a very violent, abusive individual.

Enrique came to work to see me on the mid-shift and asked me if I would speak with him privately. We walked into a break area and spoke. It was then that he told me he cared a lot about me and did not want to hurt me. It was then that there was no turning back. I was in love with a man who would hurt me and abuse me just like my mother had done.

On one occasion Enrique was berating me about my sexual history and said that I should have been able to divorce myself from my past, as if I had had a really seedy lifestyle. The way he expressed it, the message was clear: since I was not a virgin when we met, I was obviously a slut and not worthy of respect. The one thing that he would never know was that he could never loathe me nearly as much as I loathed myself. Perhaps that was part of the attraction: I hated myself so much that I projected my self-loathing by choosing a man who would go on to abuse me in the manner that I subliminally wanted. Maltreatment was the only kind of attention that I had ever known, so I subconsciously chose a man who would treat me badly.

One Saturday, Enrique and his two friends from work took me to the local mall. We went into a music shop and I thumbed through the LPs, saying to myself, 'I would like this, and I would like this...' Suddenly, Enrique became very alarmed. 'Who is going to pay for that?' he asked me. He had assumed that I expected him to buy LPs for me, although I had never once indicated to him that I wished him to buy me presents. I was so unnerved by Enrique's reaction to my innocent comments that I stopped looking at the records. As far as I was concerned, the trip had been ruined.

My work in the Electronic Maintenance section was not going well either. I was assigned to a really huge section with lots of equipment, and it was too much equipment for me to take in and try to learn all at once. I was able to work on the voice frequency carrier terminals, or VFCTs, but almost everything else was a mystery to me. My boss was having marital difficulties and had a serious problem with women in the military. He was always denigrating and insulting me in front of other people, so I stayed away from him as much as possible. As a result, my training suffered.

Before Enrique could go to Turkey, he was first required to attend training at Keesler Air Force Base, Mississippi' to study the tropospheric scatter radio system he would be maintaining. Consequently, we had only two months together before he would be going to Turkey for a year. For an 18 year old, a year was a really long time.

Enrique decided to spend Christmas in Maryland and to go to Lawrence for the New Year. I was still in denial about my family situation, and therefore decided to make plans to see my family for the New Year. I don't know whatever made me think that I could go back to Little Rock and play happy families. No sooner had I arrived than my mother lined up a major confrontation, with a little help from her girlfriends, of course.

My mother was upset that I had told one of her girlfriends, Lela, how unhappy I was with her because of some of the things she said and did to me as a child. Lela wasted no time in phoning my mother and recounting the conversation I had had with her. Instead of my mother's hanging her head in shame for having abused and neglected her children, she adopted a stance of self-righteous indignation. As soon as I arrived, she and Janet, her girlfriend at the time, confronted me with what I had said to Lela in a moment of weakness. My mother's confidence was bolstered by her new lover, so she felt no need to apologise for her actions or try to speak reasonably about all of the problems in our relationship. As a result, my trip to Little Rock was ruined because Mama, Janet and Bill just ignored me.

In desperation, I asked Anita, someone who I thought was a friend, if I could stay with her, and she refused my request even though she could see very clearly that I did not want to go home and had nowhere else to go. I was so upset with Anita for turning her back on me at that moment of need that I never spoke to her again.

For want of an alternative, I flew back to Maryland after only three days. I honestly don't know what on Earth motivated my mother to allow me to spend a significant amount of time and money to go and see her, and for her to reject me once again when I arrived. It would have been better for all concerned if she had simply told me not to come because she did not want to see me. That was not her style, however. She enjoyed making a scene and ruining my holiday because that was just one facet of her rather sadistic personality.

One evening, Enrique rang me and said he needed to speak to me. He came to my room and gave me a long list of things he did not like about me. His main problem was that I was not very ladylike. I was quite upset by the things he said to me. If there were so many things he did not like about me, then why was he going out with me in the first place? I had such a low self-esteem that the thought of breaking off with a man who had so many complaints about me never entered my mind. I did not have enough regard for myself not to tolerate a man's speaking to me in such a derisive fashion.

One evening when I was speaking to Enrique, I jokingly called him a 'spic'. I did not mean it as anything derogatory at all. When I was in junior high school, I took Spanish, which joined together with the French class to form a club called the 'Frogs and Spics'. My Spanish teacher was half Mexican and half American, and she was in charge of the club. She called the club 'Frogs and Spics' so matter of factly that I had no idea that Latin Americans considered it to be a racial slur.

When Enrique heard me jokingly call him something that I did not even know was an insult, he slapped me in the face. I was astonished that he would use physical violence to get his point across, but was not unused to it. Being a battered child, I was used to being beaten with switches, belts, planks of wood, and having all manner of objects thrown at me. Because I endured a life of horror throughout my childhood, I didn't bat an eyelash when Enrique slapped me in the face. I did not know that when a person uses violence, his actions will escalate. In fact, studies have shown that when a person expresses anger, he will actually become even angrier through the act of venting his rage. When he expresses happiness, however, he will become happier. Although that was the first time Enrique hit me, it would not be the last.

When Enrique went to Keesler Air Force Base, Mississippi, it was the first time of many that I would be required to say goodbye to someone I loved. While he was at Keesler, we spoke to each other almost every day on the telephone. I missed him terribly and hoped that he missed me. Apparently he did not do well on the course, which was somewhat of a disappointment considering the fact that he had done so well on previous courses.

One day when he phoned me, he asked me if I would marry him. I was overjoyed because I loved him very much and wanted only to spend my life with him. The following day, he phoned again and told me that he could not marry me. He had phoned his family and told them he was getting married, and they did not approve. His family wanted him to marry a local Puerto Rican girl whom they knew.

Although that was not the first time I had been rejected by one of my boyfriends' family, it was the first time I had the experience of having my boyfriend's family tell him whom he could and could not marry. Sadly, it would not be the last time I would have such an experience. I would learn the hard way that the world is full of men who are dominated by their mothers; and people wonder why we have so many wife beaters, rapists, murderers and paedophiles walking the streets today.

Any self-respecting woman would have broken up with a man who asked her to marry him and then withdrew the proposal because his mother would not let him get married. Sadly, I was not a self-respecting woman. The thought of breaking up after such a massive let-down never once crossed my mind. I just kept hoping and praying that Enrique would one day have a change of heart.

Enrique took two weeks leave before going to Turkey. My supervisor would not let me take leave even though I had the days saved up and I was entitled to take it. I can only assume that all of the men in my section knew something about Enrique that I had not been made privy to because they were not happy at all about my having a relationship with him. I therefore had to go to work during the day and see Enrique after work. Enrique stayed at the base airmen's quarters and we did things when I was not working.

For reasons that I do not understand, Enrique suffered from sexual dysfunction during our holiday. Rather than always being ready for sex, which was the norm, he could barely even maintain an erection. He apologised to me for what could only be described as a temporary impotence, but I felt no apologies were necessary. I wanted to be with him because I loved him, and was not bothered about sex at all.

One day while Enrique and I were together, he took me to Shakey's Pizza. I ordered a pasta dish and he ordered a pizza. When the food arrived, Enrique decided that he liked my entrée better than his own and therefore ate my meal while I had to make do with his. During the meal, he broke down in tears. For reasons I did not understand, he could not stop crying and would not tell me what it was that was bothering him. I was too naïve to have any understanding of what secrets he had that would make him break down in tears in the middle of a crowded restaurant.

I did not ask Enrique any questions but just tried to be there for him while he was in need. In retrospect, I wish that I had been more savvy and had asked more questions because Enrique obviously had some secret that was troubling him deeply. In the end, all of his secret demons remained unresolved and would go on to have a huge impact on my life.

One day while Enrique and I were staying in the BAQ, he became very belligerent towards me for no reason that I could imagine, and began saying really hateful things. I do not even remember what it was that he said, but he upset me a lot by his words. After he finished his tirade, he went into the bathroom to take a shower, content that he had hurt me yet again just with words. I was so upset by what he had said that I decided I was not going to put up with his behaviour any more. I packed my bags and left a note, telling him that I was leaving him. I then walked out the door, never to return.

Enrique heard me slam the door and rushed out to intercept me. It was so easy for him to get me to stay. Even after he had been horrible to me, I would continue to stay and have good times with him. Only a survivor of child abuse would go back to an abusive partner time and time again and actually have enjoyable times in between.

I ought to point out that Enrique said hateful, nasty things to me virtually every day, and it is not the purpose here to chronicle all of them. The incidents I have described in this work are just a small sample of the litany of abuse that I endured on a daily basis from the man I loved. In the beginning of our relationship, he regularly brought me to tears just with his words. After a while, however, his tirades no longer had such an effect on me. Certainly in the beginning, however, he hurt me greatly just with the things he said.

After a while, however, name calling and verbal slurs would not be enough to appease his sadistic inclination. As with most abusers, Enrique would need to increase the intensity of his bullying in order to get the same level of satisfaction. In many ways, abusers are like addicts. They need to harm others before they can feel okay with themselves, in the same way that heroin addicts need increasingly larger doses of the drug just to feel normal. After our two weeks together, Enrique went to Turkey. I had no idea at all if I would ever see him again. But even though he was in Turkey, I was still madly in love with him. I phoned him as much as possible because I wanted to keep in contact. I was able to telephone him on the Autovon network, which was a military communication system that enabled me to phone other bases all over the world. I would never have been able to afford to phone him if I had been required to pay for it.

I also wrote to him endlessly. I would write him letters and letters and letters. All of the love I poured out was for the most part unrequited. Enrique rarely wrote me letters, which often left me wondering if I were wasting my time. He did ring me one day each week and I was allowed to speak to him for 15 minutes. Because he was on a remote tour, he was allowed to make one morale call each week. At one point I got fed up with pouring out my love to him in the form of endless cards and letters, and just stopped. I decided that if he were not going to write to me, I was not going to write to him. After three weeks with no card or letter from me, I received a card from Enrique. In it he said that he missed my letters. That was all I needed to resume my letter-writing campaign.

Once he sent me a picture of him in traditional Turkish garb. On the back of the card he wrote, 'I hope you find happiness.' I thought that was an odd thing for him to write on the back of a picture, meant for his girlfriend. I suppose even then I knew that, although he was fond of me, he did not really love me.

I was not the only one to suffer while Enrique was in Turkey.

He apparently had stopped writing to his family as well. As a result of this, his family contacted the Red Cross, who contacted his commander. Enrique was therefore directed to take pen in hand and write his family a letter. Although he was obliged to write to his family, he was never obliged to write to me; although Enrique's parents had rights, I never had any.

Getting Married

Enrique told me that he would be taking leave in November of 1980, and I dutifully applied for leave at the same time as his. By this time, even I had become bored with loving a man who obviously did not love me back. Although I had never verbally expressed it, I decided that if Enrique and I did not get married, I would not be pursuing the relationship any longer.

I can only guess that Enrique thought he wouldn't have me under his spell much longer, so when I saw him for the first time in eight months, the first thing he said to me was, 'Marry me, Krystal.'

I was flabbergasted that Enrique would propose marriage after all this time, and replied by asking him, 'Are you sure that is what you want to do?'

'Oh yes, that is what I want,' replied Enrique. He was apparently sure that was what he wanted, but I do not know exactly when it was that he had made this decision.

One of the first things Enrique and I did was to go out and select wedding rings. We chose two simple bands to wear. I was quite amused when we purchased the rings because the sales assistant asked us why we were in such a hurry. He probably thought that it was because I was pregnant, but that was definitely not the case.

After we selected our rings, we went to the court house off base and registered to get married. We had to wait three days before we could go through the ceremony with the Justice of the Peace. Based on Enrique's earlier performance, I fully expected him to back out at the last minute, but he did not.

On 7th November 1980, when I was only 19, I married Enrique. By getting married, I had fulfilled one of my lifelong ambitions. On our wedding day, we went to dinner and then to a movie.

A couple of days after Enrique and I wed, we were walking towards the BAQ where he was staying. Enrique made a comment about our spending the rest of our lives together. As soon as the words came out of his mouth, I got a sick feeling in the pit of my stomach. Even at 19, I suppose I knew that I was not really the marrying kind. I could not imagine spending the rest of my life with anyone regardless of how much I loved them. One or two years at the most – anything else would be just too boring.

Shortly after we married, Enrique took me up to the Boston/Lawrence area, which was his home. I don't think he knew exactly how his family would react since they had specifically told him that they did not want him to marry me, even though they had never met me. We therefore stayed at the BAQ at Hanscom Air Force Base, not far from Lawrence. The next morning, Enrique got up at about 8:00am on the pretext of going to get a paper. Four hours later, he came back without an explanation for what had kept him so long. It never occurred to me to ask my new husband about his activities so I will never know exactly what he was doing that morning when he was unable to account for his time.

Enrique phoned his family and told them that we had married and, much to my surprise, they invited us to come and stay with them. They were quite bewildered that Enrique had married me against their wishes, and I knew full well that they did not want their son to marry me. Enrique's parents wanted their son to marry a nice Puerto Rican girl, something that I definitely was not and could never be. It saddens me no end that even into adulthood, parents try to manipulate their children and dictate to them what they can and cannot do. I do not understand why parents cannot allow their children to develop as individuals. I am perplexed by why parents want their children to be carbon copies of themselves.

Enrique's parents seemed nice enough and they even invited me to stay with them for Christmas, which was a very thoughtful gesture, particularly since my own family never bothered to think of me during the holiday seasons. Because I would not be spending Christmas with my own family, I accepted their kind invitation. I slept in Enrique's room, which was little larger than some walk-in closets. It was a tiny room that had a single bed, a closet, and a chest of drawers. Enrique would often stay in bed until well past noon, which was something I could not really understand. I have never been inclined to lying in bed all day long. I wanted to get up and do things. One of Enrique's first commands to me was that I should go into the kitchen and make him a sandwich. I don't think he really wanted a sandwich as much as he wanted to order me around. It seemed that being in the military wasn't enough for Enrique. He needed a wife so he could express the full force of his dominance of other human beings. I didn't want to make Enrique a sandwich because I did not know his family at all, yet I was expected to go into a kitchen that belonged to someone else and make my husband a sandwich. If Enrique had been humane, he would have gone into the kitchen with me to show me where everything was, but that was not his style. Enrique wanted to show his family that I was a good little wife who would do as she was told. We argued about this under the covers all morning, and finally, just to keep the peace and keep Enrique happy; I agreed to make him the sandwich. I went into the kitchen and met Enrique's mother. I explained to her that Enrique wanted a sandwich and she was kind enough to make one for her very obstinate son.

One afternoon when Enrique and I were at his parent's house, we sat on the couch, watching television. Out of the blue, Enrique asked me if I would stay with him for two years because he would need that amount of time to get his head sorted out. Enrique, it seemed, was using me as some sort of therapist. He seemed to think that I could help him to overcome the demons that raged within his mind and soul.

I had no idea whatever on Earth could be so bad that Enrique would need to sort his head out. I loved him and wanted to be with him, and had no intention of leaving. I did not even think to ask him what was so wrong with him that he needed to ask me to stay with him for two years. In retrospect, I wish I had.

It seems that I did not know how to behave as a married woman in that I became somewhat aggressive with Enrique whenever he upset me. It could be that my anger was aggression that had been repressed. My anger manifested itself in the odd push or tug while we were walking through the mall, and I was not even aware of it. When Enrique brought the pushing to my attention, I stopped it because I really had not been consciously aware that I had been doing it.

When Enrique and I were back at Andrews Air Force Base, Maryland, he went back to his dictatorial tactics. He decided that he wanted me to do the laundry but for one reason or another I did not want to do it on that particular day. He became very irate that I should have a mind of my own and might want to do something else, and declared, "You are my wife and you have to do what I tell you to do!"

I was absolutely amazed that he should speak to me in such a way. I thought that we got married because we loved and respected each other. I never realised that I was some kind of mindless trophy who had to do whatever my husband told me to do. Enrique and I had a very volatile relationship from the start of our marriage. We would get in fights over the most inconsequential things. I don't even remember what most of our disputes were about, which should serve as an example of how trivial most of our arguments were. I am sad to say that we got into a massive row on the day that he was supposed to leave to go back to Turkey. Instead of having a passionate goodbye kiss, he stormed out of my room in a rage.

Because I had been invited to spend Christmas with Enrique's family, I went about the task of buying Christmas presents for everybody. I bought presents for every member of Enrique's family and I do not know if he sent anyone in his family so much as a card. I personally did not receive a card or a present from my new husband. I do not recall Enrique's ever thanking me for taking the time to purchase presents for his family. I do not recall his ever thanking me for anything, now that I think of it.

My birthday was a month after Christmas and I did not receive a card or a present from Enrique on that day either. Since my birthday fell on a Saturday, I anticipated receiving my weekly phone call from him at least. I sat in the day room of the barracks all afternoon and no phone call came. Finally, when I went to work that evening, I rang Enrique on the Autovon network. He did not give an explanation as to why he did not ring me and I did not ask. He had apparently bragged to his colleagues on site that he had not used his weekly morale call to phone me on my birthday, and these individuals just could not believe it. He had obviously related the news to his colleagues as an act of bravado, but his declaration did not have the desired effect. Instead of lauding him for having done such a masterful thing to his new wife, they chastised him.

Enrique's colleagues therefore gave him their weekly morale call and insisted that he phone me the following Saturday. Therefore, the following Saturday I received three calls from Enrique because his friends had given him their calls. Those were such kind, selfless gestures of generosity that come so few and far between in a world were we are all taught to think of no one but ourselves. It is such a shame, also, that other people had to tell my husband the right and proper way to treat his wife.

I had been assigned to Lajes Field, Azores, which was not quite a remote posting by Air Force definition, but as close as one could get without being one. When Enrique and I got married, he applied for a joint-spouse assignment. Happily, he was given an assignment to Lajes Field as well, which meant that we could be together. When Enrique completed his one-year remote tour in Turkey, he flew back to the States to spend some time with his family before departing to yet another assignment. He was a day late in coming to collect me. Instead of coming directly to Andrews Air Force Base, Maryland, he decided to go to see his family in Massachusetts first. I was somewhat upset about this because he did not phone me to tell me what his plans were and for a whole day I did not know where he was.

The next day, he came and collected me, and took me to stay with his family for two weeks until we were due to fly out to Lajes Field. While we were in Massachusetts, he took me to Boston. It was the first time I had ever been in a major city, and it was a totally new experience. I had never been on a subway, I had never seen a policeman riding on a horse, and I had never seen so many people in my life!

It was also while we were in Boston that I happened to mention to Enrique that I had continued to take the birth control pill even when he was in Turkey. He became very irate and told me that if he had known that I was on the pill while he was in Turkey, he never would have married me. I felt that his comments were quite unreasonable. He seemed to think that just because I was taking the pill, I was having sex with an assortment of men, and that certainly was not true. I did not have sex with anyone the entire time I was parted from him, and I went on very few dates. To assume that I was promiscuous just because I was on the birth control pill was complete nonsense.

It was during one of our massive arguments that I demanded that he stop the car and let me out, which he did. Once out of the car, I started walking down the highway as Enrique sped off in a rage.

While walking, I took the exit ramp and found a shopping centre, which I entered. A few minutes later Enrique drove into the parking lot to find me. After several minutes I reappeared and got into the car. I was hoping that we would be able to kiss and make up after we had allowed our tempers to get the better of us, but that did not happen. Enrique stayed angry with me for days. He had a dark side to his personality that I was just beginning to get a glimpse of.

Azores High

The Azores is a group of nine islands that belong to Portugal. They are located in the North Atlantic Ocean, about 1,300 kilometres west of Portugal. They lie in the path of air and cable lines that link Europe and America.

Approximately 240,000 people live in the Azores. More people of Azorean descent live in the United States than in the Azores themselves. The most important city in the Azores is Ponta Delgada, which is located on San Miguel island.

The Azores form the peaks of a vast underwater volcanic mountain chain that extends from the mid-Atlantic Ocean from Iceland nearly to Antarctica. Earthquakes are fairly common. Much of the island is hilly and wooded, but it produces maize, grapes and citrus fruit.

Navigator Gonzalo Cabral claimed the Azores for Portugal in 1431. No one lived there when Cabral arrived. However, the Portuguese soon colonised the islands. The United Kingdom used the Azores as a naval base during World War II (1939 to 1945). Portugal, though neutral, permitted this because of an ancient treaty that allowed Britain to use the islands in time of war. The United States has a military installation, Lajes Field, which is located on Terciera Island, which means, in Portuguese, the third largest island in the group.

When the C141 military aircraft I was on touched down on Terciera Island, the first thing I noticed was the lush green vegetation. I had never seen so much greenery in all my life. Terciera Island is truly a Garden of Eden with its beautiful green mountainous landscape. Even today, I still dream of that beautiful island, and if it were not for the expense, I would love to go back there as a tourist.

I was assigned to Cinco Pico, a communication site about six miles from the base. It was a relay station that housed ground radio and radio relay equipment. I was working on teletype equipment, old tube type multiplexers and radio equipment. It was on Cinco Pico that I really learned my trade because the site was small enough to enable me to study the equipment and properly maintain it.

Enrique was assigned to Job Control on base. He was required to liaise with the Technical Control facility and other agencies to log jobs with the work centres such as ground radio, satcom and crypto, just to name a few.

Both Enrique and I were on shift work and our shifts would not necessarily coincide. Because of our work commitments, we would not see a great deal of each other.

When Enrique and I arrived on base, we were assigned a room at the BAQ until we found a place of our own. We also needed a car to get around, which was a pressing issue. The sponsorship that we received was not very good and we were pretty much left to fend for ourselves. It was when we were living in the BAQ that I received a first glimpse into just how inept Enrique was at making normal day to day decisions. I would also get a taste of his very violent nature, which had previously lain dormant in his personality.

We went around and looked at an apartment and told the landlord that we would like to take it. No one told us when the apartment would be vacated and when we would be able to move in. We were both too naïve to ask.

Therefore, instead of moving out of the BAQ as soon as the apartment was empty, we stayed there for two months. It was only when I let it slip to the manager of the BAQ that we had been living there for two months that they realised we should have moved out some time earlier. Enrique and I were summoned to the manager's office and we were told that we would not be required to pay back the money that we had been given to live in the BAQ, but we had to move into our apartment as soon as possible.

Enrique never said a word about my innocent comment that landed us in hot water, but I could see that he was seething with rage. He blamed me. He would never have dreamed, however, of looking at his own inadequacies as a husband and a provider. Deep down inside, Enrique saw it as my responsibility to provide a home for him, as his mother had in his more formative years. Somewhere in the mire of an unhappy marriage, Enrique's parents forgot to teach him that it was his responsibility, as a man, to ensure that family was organised. Because his mother took care of everything in his family, he expected me to do the same.

Before we could move into the apartment, it had first to be cleaned. The people who had lived there previously had very poor standards of cleanliness and hygiene and I was not willing to move in until it had been cleaned from top to bottom. The bathroom was particularly filthy and the toilet was completely caked with urine because it probably had not been wiped down the entire time the previous family had lived there.

I would go to the flat on my days off and before work, and would paint the wooden floors and clean the rooms. Enrique did not take any interest at all in the preparatory work and left it all to me. His behaviour set a precedent because the entire time we were together, he would not lift a finger around the house. He thought all of that was woman's work. He never took note of the fact that in addition to all of the woman's work I was doing at home, I was also going out every day and doing a man's job.

It was while Enrique and I were living in the BAQ that he started becoming physically violent towards me. He wanted sex on demand and he expected an active and willing partner. He had a reasonably high sex drive and could go for hours without having an orgasm. While many women would love a man as well endowed as Enrique, who also suffered from a sexual dysfunction that meant he could not climax, I was not overly thrilled.

One evening Enrique wanted to go to the movies and have sex both in the same evening, and I shrunk from the prospect of wearing myself out. I told Enrique that we could have sex or go out to the movies, but not both. Whenever I exerted my independence, Enrique became enraged and an argument inevitably ensued.

It was at that time that Enrique developed a nasty little penchant for domination and humiliation. He would wait until I was in the middle of undressing, for a shower or to put my pyjamas on. As soon as all of my clothes were off and I was completely naked, he would rush towards me, grab me, and throw me against the wall. After he had me where he wanted me, he would either grab hold of each wrist and pin me to the wall, or put his hands around my throat in mock strangulation. While Enrique was doing all of these things, he would distort his face in an ugly grimace and threaten me through clenched teeth.

With behaviour like that, it did not take long for me to lose something of the romantic feelings I had had for my new husband. Enrique only wanted a wife so he could have someone to order around, pay all the bills and give him sex whenever he felt the need to relieve himself. His decision to marry had little, if anything, to do with mutual love and admiration and everything to do with what he could get out of the marriage.

Enrique was not ashamed in the least about his aggressive behaviour towards women. One day when we had a row, I stormed off while we were in front of the BAQ. Because I was walking away from him, I did not see what he did while he was behind me. Suddenly he caught up with me, grabbed my arm, and spoke to me in an angry tone, although I do not remember exactly what he said.

Enrique must have behaved in a very threatening manner

because three teenage girls sitting on a wall witnessed him. From that point onward, those girls would taunt Enrique by calling him a 'wife beater' at every opportunity. I wanted to die of embarrassment, knowing fully well that what they said was true. Enrique, however, was completely unfazed. On one occasion, he even walked over the girls and said hello to them; I do not know if that was meant as a threat or as an act of friendliness. I suppose that in some sick way, Enrique was quite proud of being a wife beater. Even if I were in denial about the type of man I had married, other people were not.

We needed to get a car when we arrived at Lajes Field. Enrique did not really need one because he could easily have walked from our home to his job on the main base. I, on the other hand, worked more than eight miles away and therefore needed reliable transportation.

We purchased a car from a man who was being posted to another base with his family. I will never forget the day we bought the car because when the man drove us to the registration office, Enrique sat in the front seat and I sat in the back. After we bought it, however, Enrique sat in the driver's seat, the former owner sat in the back seat, and I sat in the front passenger seat.

If I had been brought up in a better class of family, I would have been happy enough with myself to have no need for such trivial territorial assignments such as sitting in the front seat, but sadly that was not the case. I was happy to sit in the front seat. If I had more confidence in myself, I would have told the previous owner that I would sit in the back seat while he sat in the front.

Even though I had paid for half of the car, Enrique took it as his own. If I wanted to drive our car, I had to ask his permission. Even though Enrique worked a mile at the very most from work, he insisted on taking our car to work every day. That left me without transport, so I had either to take the free bus the security guards used, or catch a lift from a colleague. My problems with transportation would inevitably lead to problems with my work, but Enrique didn't give a damn about that. As long as he was okay, he was not concerned in the least about any problems I might be having. Unfortunately, that was a theme that would resound in all of my personal relationships. I had terrible taste in men and would automatically make a bee line to the man who would treat me the worst.

When Enrique and I finally set up house together in our own apartment, it transpired that Enrique's money was for himself while my money was supposed to be used to support the family. We alternated paying the bills, such as gas, electricity and rent, but I bought all of the groceries. In my marriage, as in all of my subsequent relationships, I would invariably put more into the relationship than my partner. As a result of all of the money Enrique was saving by not helping out with the food bill, he amassed quite a little nest egg while I had almost no savings at all.

Enrique suffered from persistent dark moods and I could not understand why. He would come home from work in a terrible state. When he came home he would not even bother to take his uniform off and would just collapse on the couch. It was during these black moods that I could not even speak to him at all about anything. He would just lay there seething, not saying a word, while the demons inside him raged.

One day when Enrique came home from work, I rushed up to him to plant a huge kiss on him because I was so happy to see him. Enrique was not happy to see me, however. He pushed me away from him and shouted at the top of his lungs, 'Get off me!'

The message was clear. Enrique was not interested in the least in kissing me when he left or came home from work. I was deeply hurt and confused by this behaviour. I certainly did not expect to be treated like that by my new husband.

One day when I was standing in the kitchen preparing a meal, Enrique came in and kicked me with the full force of his body. I screamed out in pain and shock. I simply could not believe that my husband would resort to such violence. We had been having a disagreement, but as far as I could see, it certainly did not warrant such a blow.

Immediately after Enrique kicked me and saw the pained expression on my face, he fled the house. He was such a coward that he could not even stay and face the consequences of his actions. Hours later, when he returned from wherever it was that he had gone, I informed him that I would be leaving him. But of course I didn't. Being a survivor of childhood battering, I was accustomed to domestic violence. My rather austere marriage was merely an extension of my brutal childhood, so the experience was not entirely alien to me.

Shortly after arriving in the Azores, I seemed to be plagued with urinary tract infections. Most of them were so bad that I had to go to the bathroom every few minutes and the only thing that would clear the infection up was antibiotics. After a couple of such infections, I knew the signs and would therefore make an appointment to see a doctor, hoping to be given more antibiotics to cure the problem. The doctor, however, was not so quick to prescribe drugs. I would therefore be told that I had to allow my body's immune system to kick in and work. Consequently, I suffered in silence most of the time.

I have no idea why I seemed to have persistent urinary tract infections while I was with Enrique because I never had them before I went to the Azores and I have only ever had one flare up since that time, when a boyfriend insisted upon rubbing baby powder on me after sex.

Because I am not prone to urinary tract infections, I can only assume that Enrique picked up some kind of bacteria from somewhere and then passed it on to me. Although I would never have suspected Enrique of being unfaithful to me, I did read an article in *Cosmopolitan* magazine about a woman who was constantly picking up infections from her unfaithful lover. I can only assume, therefore, that Enrique was picking up germs from somebody and was then passing them on to me. If he were seeing somebody else, I will never know because we worked separate shifts and rarely saw each other socially.

When we settled in to our routine, Enrique would have sex with me on average once a week, and that is exactly what it was, sex. There was no lovemaking involved at all. That had vanished shortly after we arrived on the island. Enrique merely used me as a vehicle to relieve his physical urges in the same manner that he might defecate or urinate. As far as he was concerned, he was simply taking care of his bodily functions.

During our weekly sex sessions, I reverted to my childhood coping mechanism. I had not yet come to abhor the sexual act because it was something that I grew up with. When Enrique was on top of me, grunting, groaning, and doing what he needed to do to have a climax, I would be a million miles away. I remember one incident in particular when I was imagining making a lovely white suit for myself. I would rather be sewing than partaking of carnal knowledge, but was willing to submit to the chore, just as I had done when I was a child.

After a while, I did not even daydream while my husband was on top of me, relieving himself. I would simply black out. It would seem as if everything would really just go black. For years I thought that I had simply gone to sleep, and actually joked about it to someone in more desperate times. What happened, I would later come to realise, was much more complex than that. I had dissociated.

One day in the early hours of the morning, I woke up quite bewildered. My last recollection was that of my husband on top of me, having sex, and I had totally blacked out. Because Enrique was so violent, I thought for sure that he would beat the living daylights out of me if I dared to go to sleep in the middle of sex.

I woke Enrique up and asked him about the sex act. He told me to shut up and go back to sleep because we had had sex hours ago. If he had been aware of my dissociating or blacking out, he certainly did not let on. Perhaps he was so wrapped up in himself and his own needs that he was oblivious of me.

From very early in our marriage, Enrique preferred the company of men. He would take me to squadron or department barbecues and, as soon as he reached the front door, he would abandon me. He would usually make a bee line for a group of single men and would not even bother to introduce me to anybody. In virtually every social gathering we went to, he would leave me to make my own introductions and find people to speak to.

During one barbecue, a wasp flew into the can of coke I was drinking and it stung me as I went to take a sip. Enrique had left me sitting on my own on a bench and had gone to speak to a group of men standing nearby. When I spoke to Enrique about being stung by the wasp, he snapped at me for interrupting him. He was clearly engrossed in what the men were saying and was not interested at all that I had been stung by a wasp.

Our first anniversary went by almost unnoticed by Enrique. I had purchased him an anniversary present and had expected him to get me one, but as the day wore on, no acknowledgement of our 'happy day' came. I was clearly very upset but there was nothing I could say. It was entirely up to Enrique if he wanted to celebrate our anniversary and I could not force him to buy me presents or take me out for a meal.

Finally, at about 5:00pm, Enrique came into the house with a few presents. He had obviously had a change of heart and decided to get me something after all. Perhaps one of his friends told him he should get me something to put at least a little effort into our marriage. I will never know.

Enrique's violence would not abate. Whenever he became angry he would throw an object, such as a glass, across the room and it would disintegrate into small pieces. He would shove me, push me, try to strangle me and, when that didn't work, he would resort to emotional abuse.

One day when I was particularly alarmed about Enrique's behaviour, I told Master Sergeant Keiser, who was running Cinco Pico, that I wanted to leave my husband. The site superintendent knew that if I left my husband, he would have to get me a room in the barracks, help me move, and provide me with support that he was not prepared to give. I can only assume that this man did not see what the big deal was because domestic violence is very much a part of the culture of a military household. Because I did not get any support from my site superintendent, who should have been there for me in a time of need, I stayed with Enrique and put any thoughts of leaving out of my mind.

* * *

Domestic violence is rarely a one-off event. Abuse of power and control by one person over another is a central issue and can include all kinds of physical, emotional and sexual abuse. It includes abuse between partners and ex-partners whether married or not. Usually, victims of domestic violence are women, but occasionally men and same-sex couples are also victims.

Domestic violence may be experienced by anyone regardless of social group, age, race, disability, sexuality or lifestyle. Abuse can begin at any time, in new relationships or after many years spent together.

It is not easy to accept that a loved on can behave aggressively. Many victims may assume that they themselves are to blame, but no one deserves to be assaulted, abused or humiliated. It is never easy. Leaving an abusive relationship can be as frightening as the prospect of staying.

Every three days in England and Wales, a woman is killed in a domestic violence incident:

- One in four women since the age of 16 has suffered from domestic violence.
- In 90 per cent of incidents within families, children are in the same or next room.

- Domestic violence represents over 25 per cent of all reported violent crime (which is probably why the police don't want to get involved in domestic disputes – it would increase their workload).
- An incident of domestic violence takes place in the England and Wales every six to twenty seconds.
- Domestic violence impacts on victims, children, friends and family.

Baby Blues

Anyone who looked at my marriage would have been able to see quite clearly that it was not working. Nevertheless, my biological time clock was ticking; I wanted a baby desperately.

One evening when Enrique and I were sitting at the kitchen table, eating dinner, I told him that I would like to have a baby, which I felt was a natural progression of our relationship. Because I did not have a decent family to base my experiences on, I did not know that my marriage was not the sort of relationship that people should bring children into. Enrique was not pleased with my request at all and promptly locked me out of the house, hoping that I would come to my senses. I was so naïve that I thought men married for love. It never crossed my imagination that a man would marry for money, sex, or a nicer standard of living. Of course, Enrique would not tell me this for several years, but he certainly did not love me when he married me. That is one thing I do know with certainty. There is no way on Earth he could have treated me the way he did and still love me. Like most modern men, Enrique married me so he could receive sex on demand, free meals, and a highly subsidised living arrangement that he would not have been able to enjoy as a single man. Babies were definitely not on his agenda. He would stay with me as long as it suited him, but as soon as being with me was no longer economical or advantageous, he would move on.

Even though I knew that Enrique did not want to have any children, I decided to stop taking my birth control pills. To allay suspicion, I continued to have my prescriptions refilled and would merely put each tablet down the sink each morning.

I am not the most fertile of individuals, however, and even without contraception, it still took me almost a year to get pregnant, which is indicative of an internal hormonal problem. I believe I inherited polycystic ovarian syndrome from my grandmother, which means that I would always have difficulties conceiving.

Although I was quite happy living in our little apartment, Enrique got it into his head that he wanted to buy a house. I was not particularly keen on the idea because I did not want to go through the effort of moving. Enrique assured me that he would take care of the house purchase and the move, and I would not have to do any of the work involved in such a major project. He promised me that I would not have to do a thing. Like most men, he was full of promises he had no intention of keeping.

If there is one thing that Enrique was not, that was a gentleman. A classic example was one day he and I had to go to commander's call. Although Enrique worked on base, he insisted on taking the car while I had to make my way to the meeting.

After the meeting Enrique was supposed to give me a lift home, but before we left, I popped into the ladies' room. Enrique could not even be bothered to wait for me and drove off and left me at the NCO Club. When I went outside, he was nowhere to be found. I waited for him a few minutes and then rang his work. I was quite annoyed when he answered the phone. He knew he was supposed to have taken me home, but instead he chose to abandon me. An argument ensued and he angrily agreed to come get me. He sped into the parking lot of the NCO Club, sped home, and dropped me off. I was angry with my husband for just leaving me like that and he was angry with me for expecting him to behave as a reasonable husband would. When he sped off after dropping me off, I was so upset that I threw my lunch box at the car. That public act of defiance was all I could do. If I did anything else he would start beating me, and I knew it.

I was not the only person whom Enrique picked fights with.

One day when we drove to the Base Exchange, a man took the parking place that Enrique intended to park in. Enrique got out of the car and began yelling obscenities at the man, who angrily pulled out of the place. I cannot even begin to explain just how embarrassed I was. It was bad enough that Enrique behaved like a brute in his own home, but he did not even have enough self-control to behave reasonably when we went out in public.

Enrique also took a dislike to one of the waiters in the NCO Club. I do not know why he did not like this man, but when we went to the club for dinner he insisted on having another waiter. We therefore had to move tables so Enrique could have another waiter, even though I personally do not know what difference it made who we had as a waiter. I was very embarrassed at such a public display of belligerence, but that was just one of many incidents of being embarrassed by Enrique's public displays of violence and aggression.

Finally, after almost a year, I fell pregnant. When I was late on my period for exactly two weeks to the day, the morning sickness began. It is incorrect to say that I had morning sickness, because I was sick morning, noon and night. I could not keep any food down for several months, and when I was five months pregnant I still weighed less than I did when I fell pregnant. For me, pregnancy was a physically exhausting experience and I was physically ill for the entire gestational period.

When I told Enrique that I was pregnant, he was so angry with me that he told me that he would never touch me again. He complained bitterly to anybody and everybody who would listen and made it perfectly clear to me and to everyone that he did not want a baby. Enrique complained so vociferously to his colleagues that they had to tell him that he should be happy he had it in him to sire a child because there were many men who were either impotent or sterile and therefore could not have any children. It is strange to think that Enrique was so opposed to having children in view of his later behaviour. I believe that he changed his mind about wanting children when he realised they were easier to control than women. At the time, however, he was so upset that I was pregnant that he asked me to have an abortion. I was shocked that he would suggest such a thing. I told him that I was not going to have an abortion but that he was free to leave any time he liked and he would never see me or my baby again. I can only suppose that on a psychic level Enrique knew that he would not make a suitable parent. In retrospect, I wish I had the foresight to know that my husband was not an appropriate partner, provider and father.

Enrique never once brought up the subject of an abortion again. I think that he was quite surprised that for once I stood my ground. I had usually done what other people wanted me to do. I had been the perfect wife for Enrique; I was his doormat and slave. I am sad to say, though, that as soon as I got what I wanted, which was to be pregnant, I had no further need of Enrique. I suppose that attitude began to emerge as time went on. It is not as if my husband had ever been there for me emotionally or mentally. He was barely there physically. All he did was provide the sperm. He never indicated to me that there was any love involved in our lovemaking, or in our relationship for that matter.

Enrique found a house and decided to move into it when I was in my first trimester of pregnancy and in the height of the morning sickness. I was not given any time off for the move, so when I finished working a mid-shift, I had to spend all day packing, moving house and unpacking: all when Enrique had promised me that I would not have to do a thing when we moved. I was physically exhausted and I am sure the stress of the situation did nothing for the baby growing inside me.

When we moved into the new house, which was significantly larger than the apartment we had rented, Enrique still refused to lift a finger either inside or outside of the house. I was therefore left to do all of the cooking and cleaning, as usual. Even though I worked full time and took care of the house, that was still not enough for my husband, who never helped out around the house and spent all of his money on himself. He complained bitterly about my lack of domesticity, and in particular, did not like the fact that the furniture was not dusted to his specifications. If it meant that much to him, he could have dusted the furniture himself. Enrique would never do that because he considered dusting women's work.

Enrique, ever the incompetent, could not even arrange to sell the water heater. When we moved out of the apartment, the landlord offered to buy the water heater from him. Enrique waited several months to go and collect the money for it. By then, our former landlord, always looking to profit from the American presence, had decided to claim that the water heater was his and refused to give Enrique the money. Of course this behaviour was despicable, but Enrique should have made sure he had the money before we moved. That one incident is just one of many that reflects what a major fuck-up my husband really was.

It was also while we were living in the new house that the darker side of Enrique's personality began to manifest itself with an even greater intensity. For no reason that I could think of, he would lie in bed all day long. Sometimes he would not emerge from the bedroom until 4:00pm, giving me no reason whatever for his needing to hide away in the bedroom, safely under his covers. I could not understand what the matter was but I would never have dreamed of asking him.

It was also when we moved into the house that Enrique's mind games took on a more sinister tone. On more than one occasion he resorted to sleep deprivation techniques, particularly appalling since I was carrying his child and needed all the rest I could get.

One instance sticks in my mind. I was working a mid-shift and my circadian rhythm was all out of synch because I had to work five-day, swing or mid-shifts and then get one day off. The United States Air Force has never heard of the European Working Time

Directive, and as a result I had quite often to work many more than the standard 48 hours a week.

In addition, I was not given any special privileges because I was pregnant. If anything, I was made to do more work because my misogynistic bosses derived some sort of pleasure from harming my unborn child. I was not allowed to go to medical appointments, which meant that I did not receive much-needed antenatal care. I would be made to paint the site in an unventilated and unsafe area, thereby subjecting my unborn child to toxic fumes. My supervisors would also schedule me to perform training sessions during the day and then force me to go out and work a mid-shift, even when I was given a waiver that said that I could not work more than eight hours in a day. My supervisors were not concerned in the least about the well-being of my unborn child. I believe they were such sick, twisted individuals that they would have been pleased if I had miscarried as a result of the extra work I was given to do and the emotional stress that they subjected me to.

Twenty years later, living in the United Kingdom, I am amazed that my superiors in the United States Air Force were allowed to deny me pre-natal care, force me to work around toxic fumes, and force me to work unreasonable hours. In the United Kingdom, if an employer behaved the way the United States Air Force behaved, he would face litigation or an industrial tribunal. On 3rd September 2003 the *Daily Express* printed the following article:

> A dental nurse has won a tribunal against the boss who made her life so unbearable when she became pregnant that she resigned.
>
> The hearing found that Allen Branley, who owns the dental practice, bullied Vicky Matheson and effectively forced her to quit. Now Mr Branley, also a local councillor, has been ordered to pay compensation. Miss Matheson, 22,

quit in March last year claming sexual discrimination and unfair dismissal.

The tribunal found that the dentist made unreasonable and unjustifiable demands on Miss Matheson in an attempt to stop her attending antenatal appointments. The chairman said Mr Branley's conduct was shameful, although the tribunal also ruled that Miss Matheson had been partly to blame for her dismissal.

Mr Branley was criticized for the work environment in the practice, in South Shields, South Tyneside, which was said to present health risks to all female nurses of child-bearing age because of the radiation from X-ray machines. Miss Matheson said, '...I worked there for 7 months before I fell pregnant and everything was fine, I was enjoying my job. But the minute I told him I was pregnant that all stopped, and he was being really horrible to me. If ever I asked for any time off for a doctor's appointment or ante-natal classes, I was told no.

He would write horrible letters telling me that if I insisted on keeping my appointments he would take it as my resignation. He swore and shouted abuse at me. It was unbelievable and I decided that I just had to get out of it, so I quit...'

Miss Matheson, from Jarrow, went to work at another dental practice until her daughter Ellie, now one, was born.

The tribunal ordered the amount of compensation, which has yet to be set, will be reduced by one third because Miss Matheson had contributed to her dismissal.

Mr Branley refused to comment. His wife Jane, who is practice manager, said the ruling was '...inappropriate and unacceptable'...

On this particular evening that I had to work a mid-shift, Enrique woke me up abruptly at about 10:00pm. He was standing over me with a demonic look on his face and began ranting about the state of the house. My being pregnant, having morning sickness, having to work six days a week at all kinds of hours, and having to move house as well, meant that I was not able to unpack and clean the house to my husband's strict standards. Pity it never occurred to Enrique to lend a helping hand, but he would never do that. My husband would never lower himself to performing women's work.

I was so upset about being woken up two hours before I had to be up that I just got up and got ready to go to work. I never told a soul about what went on in my home. It was bad enough that Enrique behaved that way towards me, but I was carrying his child and he was putting his own son's health and safety at risk by treating me like a slave and depriving me of sleep. Enrique said that he loved my son, but how could he love a human being whom he tried to destroy before he was even born?

One evening, I came into work to perform my normal mid-shift and my loser of a boss, Herb Snedeker, was waiting for me. I had a particular distaste for him because his wife had recently left under rather dubious circumstances. Herb spent his free time with the airmen on site, smoking dope, which resulted in a major drug bust. Although Herb was smoking dope with everybody else, he gave evidence to Social Actions in an attempt to save his own skin, which shows just what a sleazy character he really was.

The deal Herb made with Social Actions was that he would take three weeks holiday while all of his friends whom he had been smoking dope with got busted. Unfortunately for Herb, Social Actions did not keep their part of the bargain. Instead of busting everyone on site and sending them to their prospective assignments, they red-lined their orders, took their security clearances away, and kept them on Cinco Pico while they proceeded with non-judicial punishment. Needless to say, there were a few unhappy people on site, just waiting for Herb.

Herb came back from leave believing that he had got off Scot free, assuming that his friends whom he had shopped would be well out of the way. He was greatly surprised to find they were still on site, waiting for him and not very happy. They were particularly upset about the fact that he had smoked dope with them, yet because he had cooperated with Social Actions, he was allowed to keep his rank as staff sergeant, his security clearance, and would not be receiving any non-judicial punishment.

As well as being the sort of person who would betray his friends in order to save himself, Herb was also a terrible technician and supervisor. After the incident of the drug bust, it was hard for me or anyone else on site to have any respect for him.

On this particular mid-shift, Herb sat in his uniform and waited for me. He went though my training records and disqualified me on all of the minor administration tasks, saying that I had said that I knew how to do them when really I did not. He didn't dare disqualify me on any tasks relating to the communication electronic equipment I worked on because he was a totally inept technician who barely knew what an electron was, much less how it worked in a circuit.

Later, when I had finished my shift and was ready to go home, I was summoned to Keith Holshouser's office. Holshouser, who was the site superintendent at the time, had a letter of counselling prepared for me, which no doubt had been typed up in advance.

I was upset about Keith and Herb's antics because I was tired from having worked all night and angry about having been disqualified on all of those tasks. I was also pregnant and suffering from morning sickness, and all I wanted to do was go home and go to my bed. I was very forthright with Keith and did not hesitate to let him know that I was not happy at all about what he and Herb were doing.

Because I was upset, Keith played one of the oldest tricks in the book. He asserted that I was mentally unstable and made me see a psychiatrist that very morning. Nothing whatsoever was said about the fact that I was on a waiver and was not supposed to be working more than eight hours in one day. I did not have any rights and was made to go along with whatever the commander, first sergeant, and Keith Holshouser wanted.

When Keith drove me to the hospital, his words to me were, We are only trying to help you. I have no doubt that many an abuser has said that very same thing to a victim just before inflicting pain, and sometimes even death.

I looked at Keith as if he must be crazy. If Herb and Keith were trying to help me, I wonder what they would have done if they had malice on their minds. I knew that Herb and Keith were misogynists who both had failed marriages. They did not think women should be in the military and therefore tried to use military channels to destroy me. To say that I was mentally unsound was just an attempt to get rid of me because they both knew that they could never fault my work.

It is worth noting that for centuries men have been putting women away in mental institutions when they wanted to get rid of them. It is such a shame that Herb and Keith came up with such an unoriginal idea. Otherwise, they might very well have succeeded. What really saddens me is the fact that while they were using the military institution to harass me, they never gave a thought to how their actions might affect my unborn child.

Therefore, instead of resting, which is what I so desperately needed, I was made to sit in the hospital so a psychiatrist could speak to me and decide whether I was crazy or not. Thankfully, the psychiatrist was a very reasonable person. She said that there was nothing wrong with me at all. She said that because I was pregnant, my hormones were flaring up, and that was making me more emotional.

Finally, at about midday, I made it to my bed. I could not sleep, though, so I just passed out and waited for Enrique to come home from his nice, cushy day job at Plans and Scheduling. Enrique had heard something had happened, but he was not bothered enough to see if I were okay. He instead demanded that I tell him what happened as soon has he finished work at 5:00. When he found out what Herb and Keith had done, he became enraged, not so much, I believe, out of concern for my well-being as because both of those individuals were laughing stocks on the main base, which is why they were working at Cinco Pico. I can only suppose that Herb allowed himself to become involved in Keith's plan as a way to salvage what little was left of his reputation after the drug bust several months earlier.

Enrique decided the following Monday we both would go speak to the first sergeant about what happened the previous Friday. It was during this meeting the first sergeant informed me that Herb and Keith had approached him with a view to denying me my NCO advancement, which would be coming up shortly. Since I had no record of disciplinary problems whatsoever, Herb and Keith decided that they would fabricate one, which is why they disqualified me on all those tasks, gave me a letter of counselling, and sent me for a psychiatric evaluation in the hope that I would be regarded as emotionally unstable.

After our meeting with the first sergeant, we went to see the section commander. The person whom we were supposed to see was on holiday, so we saw a stand-in. It appeared that he was on friendly terms with Herb and Keith, and was more than willing to go along with them in anything they wanted to do.

The fact is that when I was in the office alone with Keith, I asked him to give me specific examples of things I had done that made him believe I should not be an NCO, and he was never able to give me a concrete answer. The simple fact was that he did not like me because I was a woman, and that was all the information he felt he needed to deny me NCO status. Keith and Herb didn't think women should be in the military, and they certainly didn't think women should be non-commissioned officers.

After the somewhat negative meeting with the stand-in section commander, I went to see the Inspector General to discuss the problem. This one was a good deal more positive. The IG noted that I could not be denied NCO status just because someone did not like me. They had to have concrete evidence, which they were not able to come up with, no matter how hard they tried. Herb and Keith were instructed to do their job properly, and that is something they did not like at all.

Because I had been disqualified on all of those tasks, I had to work the day shift with Herb so he could train me, which was a joke, really. This put pressure on the rest of the site because other people had to work the shifts that I could not work. Herb tried his best to train me, but considering the fact that I knew the job better than he did, it really was a pointless endeavour. He did not know the first thing about radio relay equipment repair, and he certainly couldn't supervise. The best leadership is by example, and Herb and Keith were not very good examples of NCOs. If anything, they taught others how not to treat people.

I was finally summoned in to the office of the section commander. He told me they had decided to give me NCO status, but he had a little message for me. He said, 'The battle isn't over yet.'

I had no idea what that message was supposed to mean. I did not know if he were speaking on behalf of Herb and Keith, or if he were reflecting the sentiments of higher powers. I personally thought it was an inappropriate and offensive thing to say. The command section was worried that they might face repercussions for what they had done, and therefore decided the best thing to do would be to remove me from Cinco Pico, where I was still being harassed by Herb and Keith. I was therefore sent to work at Job Control on the main base, where Enrique had previously worked.

It was also during that very dark time in my life when Enrique told me that I should get out of the Air Force and go to live with him in Lawrence. I did not want to do that, however. Enrique had almost total control over me while I was in the Air Force and I dreaded to think what would happen if I had no job, no money, and a baby to support. I also knew in my heart that when Enrique had me where he wanted me, the violence would increase and would eventually become unbearable. I declined Enrique's rather self-centred offer. The military was not an ideal situation, but at least I had a little bit of independence. With Enrique, I would have no independence whatsoever, and that is something I knew beyond a shadow of a doubt.

When I was working in Job Control my supervisor told me that I had to attend a meeting with Social Actions. I had no idea what the meeting was about, but when I got there the room was full of enlisted females. From what I gathered, there was a great deal of dissatisfaction amongst the women on base, as they all seemed to have a particular gripe about one thing or another.

A young black woman complained about the way she had been treated when she was pregnant. When she was given a waiver to work only eight hours a day, she was made to report for work at 4:00am in the morning. She would have been really unhappy if she had worked at Cinco Pico because I was required to work a day shift and then turn around and work a mid-shift. I was also not given time off to attend doctors' appointments.

It was during this meeting that I voiced some of the things that went on at Cinco Pico. I told them about all of the things that were said to me, and specifically some of the things that Keith Holshouser had said. When I told Social Actions that Keith told me that oriental women do not have any pubic hair, they were incredulous. When I told them that Keith told me I should shave my pubic hair because I would love it and my husband would love it, they got their notepads out and began writing things down. An investigation ensued regarding Keith Holshouser's sexual harassment of me. The military authorities were concerned about what Keith had said, but I was much more offended by his behaviour.

Keith would call me the 'woman of the hour', which was calculated to annoy. He would intentionally get my rank wrong on military documents, he would order me to perform absurd tasks and he would make me perform the same tasks over and over again, telling me that I was not going to be given any special privileges because I was a woman. I never once asked for any special privileges. I just wanted to be treated the same as my colleagues, nothing else.

Of course Keith denied everything, as he would. He also went home to his wife and gave her a fabricated story about why he was being investigated. The story Keith told his wife alarmed her so much that she told everyone who would listen that she was going to sue me for causing her husband stress. Somehow, during all of the turmoil that ensued, nobody seemed to give the slightest thought to the stress my unborn child and I might be going through.

One may wonder what happened to the bond between Herb Snedeker and Keith Holshouser that seemed so strong at the time they were hell bent on destroying me as an effigy to all womankind. Well, as one might guess, as soon as I was out of the picture they became bitter enemies. Apparently, they had become friends in the first place through their shared dislike of women and the opportunity to work together to cause me damage. They were similar, admittedly, in other respects as well. Both were overweight, over the hill losers who would only ever be able to get jobs as security guards in the real world. They were not worthy to wear the uniform.

It was also during the investigation that it was decided that Keith Holshouser would be sent down to the main base to work in Quality Control. I was particularly upset about this because I had left Cinco Pico to get away from him, and now he was being sent down to work in my department. I suppose that Keith left Cinco Pico in a cloud because he was not particularly well liked and he was certainly not respected. He was in for a big surprise because while he had been in a position to demand superficial respect on the site, that would not be the case on the main base.

Because Keith Holshouser would be working in my department, it was decided that I would be transferred to the Wideband Maintenance work centre. Within a matter of months, I had been sent to work in two departments, just to get away from that man.

Enrique was still as controlling as ever. He even told me what clothes I could and could not wear. He did not like me to wear the colour red because he believed that only loose women or prostitutes wore red. Therefore, when I made a red maternity dress, Enrique did not want me to wear it because he believed that people would think I had loose morals. The fact that I was heavily pregnant and few men would be interested in me was of no consequence.

Because Enrique was a loose cannon, ready to explode at the slightest provocation, I knew better than to defy him in any way because he would not hesitate to resort to violence. As a result of this, I had to repress much of the anger I felt inside. This unbridled anger no doubt affected my relationships socially and professionally because I now know that there are very few people who can dissociate themselves from their problems at home. If I had had a happier home life then I might very well have had a happier social and professional life. Since I had never had a happy home life, I had no frame of reference to judge my life by and, as amazing as it sounds, I had no way of knowing just how deeply unhappy I was.

Because Enrique was bigger and meaner than me, I did not dare confront him or even stand up for myself for that matter. Such tactics would have only led to more unbridled violence and I would have been the one to get hurt. Therefore, whenever I was angry with my very belligerent husband, I would take a pair of scissors and cut up his underwear, ties, or anything else I could find. Although I would never admit it to myself, I really wanted to cut him up, but his clothes would have to do. Enrique must have known that I cut up his clothes when I was angry with him but he never said one word to me about it. I suppose that even then he knew that I cut up his clothes, but he cut up my soul. One could always go out and get a new outfit, but getting a new soul was a different matter entirely.

The rage within Enrique would not abate. He seemed to be particularly angry when he came home from work, although I don't know what interchange he had with other people to put him in such a foul disposition. One evening in particular he came home while I was fixing dinner. He sat on the couch, scowled at me, and yelled, 'What are you looking at?' before grabbing the closest object he could find and hurling it at me.

I was so astonished that my husband would make such an unprovoked attack that I just stood there in front of the stove, speechless. It never occurred to me to think that Enrique's behaviour was abnormal because in my mother's house I was regularly called names, hit with any available object, and had things thrown in my direction.

With all-day morning sickness, problems at work and problems at home, I somehow forgot to eat. Therefore, when I was five months pregnant I weighed less than I did when I fell pregnant. Although Enrique did not want a baby and took no interest in my pregnancy, he announced that he was not happy about the fact that I was not gaining weight.

Always eager to please, I started eating. By the end of the pregnancy, I had gained almost 50 pounds. People believe that when a woman is pregnant, she is eating for two. They encourage her to stuff herself and gain lots of weight, thinking that is what the baby needs. In reality, it is better if the woman does not gain too much weight because the more weight she gains, the more she will have to take off after the baby is born.

Thanks to Enrique, I would develop an obsession with my weight. That was nothing new, however. When I was a child my mother, father and other relatives often told me how fat I was. For the first time in my life I was being told that I was not fat enough. Is it any wonder I have had an eating disorder for my whole life?

As strange as it may seem, I still loved my husband even though he did not behave in a way that warranted any kind of love or affection. One evening, on an extremely rare occasion, I decided that I wanted some intimacy. I therefore sat by Enrique, who was lying on the couch, watching television. I put my hand on his shoulder and caressed it for several minutes, hoping that he would get the message. Enrique just lay on the couch, inert, continuing to stare at the screen. It did not take me long to get the message. Enrique did not want me.

Even though I was a battered child who had survived sexual, physical and mental abuse, as well as severe neglect, if I had been fortunate enough to go on to form a relationship with a nice man and have a healthy marriage, I may very well have matured into a sexually healthy adult. The extremely dysfunctional adult relationships I went on to develop did nothing but reaffirm my highly ambivalent feelings about sex.

There is one thing I do know, and it is that Enrique had a high sex drive. I have often wondered if, during that time when he didn't want me, if he wasn't sleeping with me, who was he sleeping with?

It was while Enrique was working in Plans and Scheduling that he developed a friendship with John, who also worked there. Enrique became particularly attached to him for reasons that I do not fully understand. We would spend almost every weekend doing something socially with John and his family. Every Saturday morning, Enrique would get up early and leave the house, and I would not see him again until late in the evening. On several occasions I would have to ring John's house and ask Enrique to come home for dinner. It was quite apparent to me that Enrique had much more affection for John than he did for me, but I do not know if John returned the feelings.

When I was seven months pregnant, Enrique decided to take a holiday on his own, without me. He was gone for almost three weeks and callously timed his holiday to fall on my 23rd birthday. Therefore, instead of celebrating, I was mourning the fact that I had a straying husband who would rather be holidaying in sunny Spain than being with his wife during the last trimester of her pregnancy.

Enrique came back from his Spanish holiday safe and sound and full of presents he had purchased for me. When I asked him how he could leave me on my birthday, he said that he had to because he was afraid that he was going to go crazy. I could not understand what on Earth could make him go crazy. I didn't even have enough comprehension of the dynamics of mental illness to ask him why he thought he was going crazy.

Although I never said anything to Enrique about his abandoning me at such a crucial time, I suppose he could not help feeling guilty about it. His colleagues may very well have said something to him about his actions, but I am not aware of it. In any case, shortly after his Spanish holiday, he decided to take me on a mini-break to the island of Fayel, which was also part of the Azores. That holiday turned out to be a disaster, again because of Enrique's behaviour.

The evening we arrived, Enrique decided he wanted to take me to the local disco even though I was eight months pregnant and had a pinched nerve in my back which caused excruciating pain. The only thing that would ease the pain was to lie flat on my back, but that was difficult in the middle of a disco.

Although Enrique wanted to go to the disco, he did not want to do anything while we were there. He only wanted to sit at a table, have a drink, and watch the people. He certainly was not interested in making conversation with me: that is one thing I do know. I told Enrique several times that I wanted to leave because I was in so much pain. He, as usual, was not interested in my pain and insisted we stay, even though he sat there, holding onto his drink, not saying a word to me. Finally, when I could not stand the pain any longer, I kicked his toe with my foot and told him that I wanted to go. He stormed out of the disco in a huff and did not speak to me for the rest of the trip. Although Enrique's rejection of me upset me deeply, I was so accustomed to it that I didn't think twice about it. Enrique had treated me so badly for such a long time that not only did I not expect to be treated in any other way, I would not know what to do if a man ever did decide to treat me well.

Within five minutes of arriving back from our mini-break, Enrique was on the phone to his friend, John. It was quite apparent that Enrique had much more feeling for his colleague that he would ever have for me.

Childbirth – An Unhappy Event

On 7th April 1983, I woke up at about 5:45am with severe pains in my back. My child was overdue. I knew he was, but the military doctors said that he was not due for another two weeks.

Because I had back pains, I did not think I was in labour. I was expecting to have pain in my stomach, which is the most common type of labour. I therefore put my uniform on and prepared to go to work because in the United States Air Force I was not allowed to have any time off work just because I was having a child.

As we were preparing to go into work, however, it was decided that because my labour pains were at regular intervals I should go to the hospital. Our car had broken down and Enrique had never bothered to get it fixed, so his friend John gave me a lift to the hospital.

When I was in the maternity ward I was told to take all of my clothes off and put a gown on. The nurse then put a huge speculum inside of my vagina so she could examine me. The object the nurse inserted in me was so large that I flinched and yelled out from the pain. The nurse chastised me and told me not to be such a baby. It was later revealed that the speculum that she inserted into me was an extra large, and I only needed a small. The object was so large that it actually cut me and I was bleeding. No one ever apologised. There seemed to be some confusion as to how far I had dilated. After two nurses and one doctor inserted their massive hands in the birth canal, it was finally agreed that I had dilated 4cm.

After it was determined how much my cervix had dilated, I was told to put my clothes on and go into an office to speak to a doctor. Dilated 4cm, and in labour, I sat in front of the doctor, wearing my maternity uniform, while he told me that I must go back to work. I looked at the man in complete astonishment.

But I am in labour, I managed to stammer to the doctor.

I know you are in labour, but you have not dilated enough and I cannot release you from work, said a rather stern doctor who was no doubt being ordered not to give women time off work just because they just happened to be giving birth. The simple fact that I was ordered to go back to work while I was in the middle of giving birth is a clear indication to me that the American armed forces is a misogynistic, woman-hating organisation. Who else would order a woman in labour to go back to work?

I rang my work in tears and explained to them that although I was in labour, the doctor was still sending me back to work. I did not want to sit at work, in labour, and I am sure that my colleagues did not want me to go to work whilst I was in the middle of giving birth.

The person who picked up the phone was understandably horrified. Nobody in that section wanted me there that day regardless of the fact that the United States Air Force had a policy that women must report for duty until the exact moment that their baby actually comes out of their body. I felt guilty for letting the military down and relieved that I did not have to go to work and subject my colleagues to my suffering. I therefore went home even though I had been ordered to go back to work.

The minute I got home I took my uniform off and put on some comfortable clothes. By this time the contractions were five minutes apart, yet I still felt guilty for not being at work. After being at home for about an hour and not having any respite from the pain, I phoned the hospital and told them that I really was in a lot of pain and the contractions were five minutes apart. The nurse reluctantly told me that if I was in that much pain then I could go back in, but I got the distinct impression that she did not believe me. Back in the maternity ward, unclothed and having yet another vaginal examination, it was determined that the previous examination was incorrect. I had dilated 6cm and not 4cm!

The doctor decided that in an attempt to speed up the labour process, I should walk up and down the corridor. Therefore, hanging on to an IV, I walked up and down the hallway for almost an hour. It was not very pleasant, however, because I was having back pains and it was difficult for me to stand during a contraction.

The nurses then decided that I should go back to the bed and lie down. The doctor came in to examine me and told me that I would have my baby in a couple of hours. That was at about 4:00pm.

He then decided to break my water. When the water came out it was green, which was not a good sign. The green water, or luconiam, meant that my baby had had a bowel movement while still in the womb. The excrement was toxic and if the baby inhaled it or swallowed it, he could be very ill.

Due to the severity of my baby's condition, it was decided that even though I was in excruciating pain, I would not be given any anaesthetic. The reason for this was because anaesthetic would slow down my baby's heart beat and other bodily functions, which would pose problems if he did ingest any of his own excrement. The doctors wanted me to be fully alert when he was born because they wanted to take every precaution that I would have a healthy baby.

The doctor wanted to monitor my baby's heart beat, and put a monitor on my stomach. It was impossible to get an accurate reading, however, because I had a layer of fat around my middle, the result of a hormonal problem that I inherited from my grandmother. The doctor therefore decided to place the monitor on the baby's head, so yet another object was inserted inside me.

The hours went and the contractions intensified, but there was still no baby. At one time I became nauseous and had to vomit a yellow substance called bile into a tray. I told the nurses several times that I was thirsty, but I was given nothing to drink. Finally, I was allowed to suck on a damp tissue.

It was during this very intense labour that Enrique decided that he wanted to leave to get some dinner. I looked at my husband in horror.

'Don't leave me!' I begged. The pain was so unbearable that I became delirious. I started begging the nurse to kill me because I simply could not handle the pain any longer. Not only did I feel as if my back were going to break, but this time my pelvic bone had to spread in order to accommodate a large baby.

The nurse, who was the same one who injured me by inserting the extra large speculum into me, sternly told me to pull myself together. She was certainly not tolerating any hysterics on her shift. I suppose that in a way she was right because I needed all of my energy for giving birth, not for screaming bloody murder.

Hours passed and there was still no baby. The doctors felt sorry for me and decided that I could have a mild painkiller, which was the equivalent of Tylenol III. This drug only lasted about an hour, however, and after that I was on my own.

While all of this was going on I discovered that I was not able to urinate. The doctor therefore inserted a catheter into my urinary tract to enable me to pass fluid.

In late evening there was still no baby, even though I had been assured that I would have my baby by early evening. At 10:00pm I was told that I had dilated 10cm, and even though I wanted to push, I could not. I don't know all the details, but the doctor said that the time was not yet right to push.

After not being allowed to push for what seemed like an eternity, I was told by a male nurse that I could push. I was therefore taken to the delivery room and told to push during each contraction.

The problem was that I had been through a very traumatic experience. I had been in labour since before 6:00 that morning, had gone to work, and then had to go to the hospital. While at the hospital the nurse used incorrect instruments to examine me and injured me in the process, and when I cried out in pain she called me a baby. The nurses had not accurately detected how much my cervix had dilated and, as unbelievable as it sounds, I was told to go back to work by another doctor. My work section, not the doctor, told me to stay home because my colleagues certainly did not want to be around a pregnant woman in the throes of labour. I was then grudgingly allowed to go back to the hospital, even though it was not believed that I was in fact in labour. I was not given anything to eat or drink all day long, had to endure a horrendous labour all on my own, bar one 45 minute mild painkiller. I had suffered many hands inside of my body all day long. In addition to that, my blood pressure had shot up to extremely high levels.

I pushed and pushed and pushed for at least 45 minutes, and there was still no baby. After such an arduous experience, I collapsed. I simply could not push or move or do anything that I was told to do any longer. They could not make me push because I simply had no more energy left. I suppose the doctor felt that I had been pushed to the limit, so he got his trusty forceps out.

Although I had been given an episiotomy, the forceps and the baby's large head totally ripped through my birth canal and back passage. After it was all over, there was not much left of me.

The baby came into the world face up. He may very well even have had the umbilical cord wrapped around his neck, but I cannot honestly remember whether or not that was the case. Because almost every bone in my baby's body was double jointed, his back formed an extremely sharp backward arch, which meant that he had formed an odd position while he was in the womb.

Because my baby was born face up, many people of a religious or spiritual ilk believe that he will have spiritual qualities as an adult because he was born facing God.

The nurses thought he was lovely. He had a full head of dark brown hair and they commented on his chubby little thighs. The nurses said that because the skin on his fingers was cracked, he was about a week late. My estimates, therefore, of his ideal birth date were correct, while the doctor's estimates were off by three weeks. They had projected that the birth should occur on 21st April, while I believed that it should have occurred on 1st April.

The baby had an apgar score of 9 and was very healthy indeed. It was I who was the total wreck. After I gave birth, the doctor decided that it was time to sew me up, and there was a lot of stitching to do. They had to completely reconstruct a new vagina and back passage since both had been ripped out during the delivery.

It was only when the doctor was reconstructing my private parts that I was allowed a local anaesthetic, but I still felt every single stitch. The doctor wanted to give me more stitches, but I begged him not to. I absolutely hated what he was doing to me because I could feel it all. I could not bear it that he had to sew me back up.

It was during the reconstruction that my doctor proudly told me that he had used every single instrument that there was to enable a woman to give birth naturally. A nurse came and told me later that she knew that I had been through a really rough time. She informed me that I had suffered fourth-degree lacerations. It had been torture. In this day and age of quick fixes and painkillers, I was made to do it all on my own. I never, ever wanted to have another baby as long as I lived.

They say there are properties in mother's milk that will make the mother forget about the birthing process, but I did not forget. I don't think there are enough chemicals or drugs on the face of this Earth that could make me forget such a difficult pregnancy and traumatic labour.

After I gave birth, Enrique came to me and said he wanted to name the baby Matthew Manuel, after my father and his father. I recoiled in horror because Enrique had obviously been listening to the men at work, who told him that he must name his child after a family member. I wanted my child to have his own identity, his own personality.

'I want my baby to be called Aaron Alexis,' I informed my husband. He was to be named Aaron simply because I liked it and Alexis because it was his father's middle name. As I would later come to realise, the naming of my baby was one of the few decisions that I would ever be allowed to make regarding his destiny. One of the others was my insistence that he not be circumcised. I saw it as an unnecessary procedure that would only cause him pain. One of the nurses commended me on my independent thinking because so many mothers simply go along with convention and never question whether a certain procedure is right for them.

Enrique felt sorry for me, which should serve as a clear indicator of what a really difficult time I had. He told me that I should sleep in the following morning and take it easy, which was about the only bit of sympathy he would ever give me. I did not get to sleep in, however, because at 5:00 the following morning, a nurse made me get up, shower, and walk around a bit.

I was the only person in the maternity ward that week and was very lonely. I do not recall if Enrique came to see me every day, but he certainly did not stay long when he did visit. He also did not bring me flowers, which I understand is customary and would have liked.

I was kept in hospital for five days. They would not allow me to go until I had a bowel movement because my insides were so badly damaged. I was eventually allowed out, but only on the strict condition that I go home and get as much rest as possible. I did not know it at the time, but the doctors and nurses must have been very concerned about me.

As I was leaving the hospital, I carried my own suitcase. The nurse chastised me and Enrique, saying that after what I had been through I should not be lifting anything heavy. The nurses could see how ashen my face was, which reflected the total exhaustion that I still felt from a very difficult pregnancy and excruciating labour. The only reason I was allowed to leave at all was because I kept pestering the doctor, asking him when I would be allowed to go home.

When I got home, I was in so much pain that I could not leave the house. Enrique had to go the Base Exchange and buy me some new clothes because I did not have any in my wardrobe that fitted.

My hips were really too small to give birth naturally, but because I was young and Aaron was double jointed, he managed to squeeze his way though my small hips and birth canal, which flexed and tore to accommodate him. My rib cage had been much smaller as well, but his body growing inside of me forced it to bend to his expanding body as well. Although my bone structure was really not large enough to accommodate my baby, because I was so young, my bones moved out of his way so that he could have life. But after giving birth, my body would never, ever be the same again.

Because I was too ill to leave the house, Enrique took it upon himself to go to the CBPO, which was a unit that took care of personnel administration, and registered Aaron as his dependent. That one act alone meant that Enrique would receive all the extra money and entitlements for having a dependent. That was just one of many things Enrique would do to undermine my authority as Aaron's mother.

One day Enrique came home with an unwrapped gift from Keith Holshouser. I simply couldn't believe the nerve of that man, after all he had done to harm me and my baby, and he was buying him presents!?! Keith Holshouser was totally unbelievable. I asked Enrique why he accepted the present and he could not answer me. I told Enrique that I didn't want any presents from that man in my house, so he ended up throwing it in the garbage can outside. Enrique would never stand up to Keith Holshouser, or any man for that matter.

Even though I had been through a horrendous ordeal, I was expected to walk Aaron down to the hospital all on my own. Sometimes I barely managed it; walking was still a painful ordeal. I coped. I managed to walk to the base and back while my husband sat in his office, pretending to be the big man. If he were truly a big man, he would have helped me a little, but he would never lower himself to do anything for a woman – even if that woman happened to be the mother of his child.

Even though Enrique told anybody who would listen that he did not want a baby and he was very angry with me for falling pregnant, as soon as Aaron was born he underwent a personality change: he took Aaron over, body and soul, which is not what I wanted. I was Aaron's mother, yet I had no say in his upbringing. I could not even decide what clothes he could wear. He had a lovely outfit that had a duck on it, but Enrique said that he could not wear it because ducks had homosexual overtones. Now, how on Earth can a small baby be perceived as a homosexual just because he is wearing an outfit that has a duck on it? It reminded me of Enrique's insistence that I would be perceived as a prostitute if I wore a red dress when I was heavily pregnant. I never really thought about it at the time, but Enrique had some really strange ideas.

In retrospect, I do not think that Enrique ever really loved Aaron because he is not capable of love. He just saw Aaron as someone else he could control, a small person whom he could manipulate and force to do whatever he wanted him to do. How could Enrique possibly love Aaron? A man who loves his child does not deprive him of a mother.

On 3rd November 2002, the *Daily Mail* published an article, 'Childbirth: An Unhappy Event'. The article highlighted the fact that for some women, childbirth can be a traumatic experience. Although science and technology have improved since the days when women regularly died in childbirth, there are still all sorts of factors that can make for a traumatic experience: unsympathetic midwifery staff, poor pain control, or the unnerving loss of control when events take an unexpected turn for the worse.

They say that the hormone prolactin, the 'bonding hormone' which stimulates the production of breast milk, is linked with forgetfulness about labour – a sort of blessed hormonally induced amnesia, which gives first-borns their siblings. A few women never forget. Some will have trouble bonding with their baby or lose their nerve so completely that they'll never risk another pregnancy; some will never again have a fulfilling sex life with their partner; others will suffer lasting unhappiness and marital breakdown. A few will go on to suffer full-blown post-traumatic stress disorder, or PTSD, experiencing the same constellation of symptoms as if they had been attacked or injured in a catastrophic car crash: abrupt mood changes, panic attacks, flashbacks, cold sweats, nightmares, crying fits, or agoraphobia. However, even though research has shown that a traumatic birth experience can cause the same level of PTSD as has been found in Vietnam War veterans, few doctors make this connection. If there are signs of psychological ill health, most doctors will link these to hormonal changes after birth, and not to anything that may have happened during it.

Gabrielle Downey, consultant obstetrician at Birmingham City Hospital (where 700 to 800 women a year give birth under her care) finds the psychological aftershocks are greatest in women for whom it was the first birth and women who had fixed expectations of the type of child they wanted and didn't get. Now we have such tight control over our everyday lives, we expect something of the same autonomy in the delivery room, she says. The birth process comes as even more of a shock to contemporary women than it did to previous generations.

When events gather momentum in an unfamiliar setting, with unfamiliar people, it is easy for even the most independently minded woman to feel lost, bewildered, bullied, fearful – not to mention disappointed and a failure if everything does not go according to plan.

One would think that the pain was the worst part of the whole experience, but psychotherapist Dr Heather Allan says that for 99 per cent of the people who consult her, pain is not the lasting issue; it's the emotional and psychological distress.

When the unexpected happens, and women are left feeling let down at best and shocked and traumatised at worst, the importance of debriefing sessions is beginning to be recognised. 'From the most wonderful to the most terrible, it's really important to talk about your birth,' says Janet Balashas, founder and director of the Active Birth Centre in North London, which encourages women to come back to the antenatal classes to share their birth experiences.

Post-natal Depression

In all of the childbirth books I had read, it was mentioned that about three days after giving birth, the new mother would feel a bit blue and would begin to cry. This was attributed to hormonal changes and this one day of tearfulness was given the name post-natal depression.

I had no experience of being sad shortly after giving birth. I had too much to do. I was pretty much a single mother because Enrique had never been there for me emotionally or materially, and he was just barely there for me physically. I had always been responsible for my own financial well-being, and having a baby never changed that. Instead of being responsible for one person, I was now responsible for two.

To be honest, I loved Aaron so much that the only feelings I had for him were adoration. It is very difficult to feel the effects of depression when the only emotion you feel is sheer and utter devotion to your baby.

Enrique knew I was totally in love with Aaron and I can only assume he decided to hurt me in a way that would completely destroy my whole being and numb my soul. Enrique would decide to use my son to harm me in an attempt to kill my soul.

Enrique became obsessed with routine. Every four hours he woke Aaron up from his peaceful slumber to feed him. Although it was an inconvenience to Aaron, it simply wore me out because I was still very weak from giving birth. I spoke to the doctor about what Enrique was doing and he assured me there was no need to wake Aaron up to feed him. Aaron would wake us up when he was hungry, I was told. Enrique was so obsessed with keeping Aaron to a routine that he actually gave him diaper rash. Every four hours, Enrique would wake Aaron and change him. He didn't bother to wear his glasses and therefore didn't clean his bottom properly. He also failed to notice that Aaron had a nasty rash developing. Even though Aaron would cry out in pain, Enrique would nevertheless put all kinds of potions and powders on him that he purchased at the Base Exchange. The following morning I got up to change Aaron and was distressed to see that he had a horrible, scabby rash on his bottom, which was a direct result of all of those chemicals that Enrique had been putting on him.

I rang the hospital and made an appointment to see a doctor, who prescribed antibiotic cream and told me to wash Aaron's bottom with water instead of using all of those nasty, chemical-laden products that Enrique had purchased.

It was at that point that I stopped using baby powder on Aaron because he was so obviously allergic to it. I was so worried the doctors would think I was a bad mother for giving my child diaper rash, but it wasn't me, was it Enrique. From the day Aaron was born I tried to do what was best for my son. My husband, however, always did what was best for himself. I could not help being angry at Enrique because he put all of those chemicals on Aaron without even noticing his allergic reaction to them.

In addition to putting Aaron on a routine rather than allowing his own circadian rhythm to take effect, Enrique would wrap Aaron in far too many clothes when he went out. At one point Aaron was so hot he actually started crying; the poor little thing was burning up. Again, I was very upset with Enrique because he had taken it upon himself to make all of the decisions regarding my son's welfare, but those decisions were for the most part clearly wrong. Enrique believed that I was an inept mother and that he knew what was best, but all of the decisions he made about Aaron seemed to be harmful.

When Aaron was five weeks old, we all boarded a C141 military aircraft to go back to the States. It was a five-hour flight and we were given box lunches to eat. Aaron was wet and I wanted to change him, but Enrique would not allow me to. He had the strange idea that it was socially wrong for me to change my baby's wet diaper on a plane. This overrode any consideration for his own son's comfort and well-being.

When we touched ground, one of the first things I did was change Aaron's diaper, which was soaking wet. I was angry and upset that Enrique would not permit me to change it on the plane, especially since he was still recovering from a nasty bout of diaper rash previously described.

When we arrived in Lawrence to spend some time with Enrique's family, he was in his element and his behaviour therefore went from bad to worse. He treated me with total disregard and would even call me names, such as 'bitch', in the presence of his two sisters, Lesvia and Maira.

One morning I decided to try on a pair of Enrique's jean shorts because I did not have many clothes to wear. Enrique stirred from his slumber to see me trying on his jeans and characteristically became enraged.

'You take them off!' my husband shouted at me in a rather gruff voice. I did as I was told because I knew that Enrique would not hesitate to use violence if necessary.

I took the jeans off and tried to repress my hurt feelings. I could not understand why Enrique was so averse to me trying on his jeans. I buried my hurt feelings and resentments deep within my being. Being a survivor of child abuse, I was well versed in the art of getting on with life and acting as if everything were normal when someone insulted me, physically assaulted me, or touched me inappropriately.

It was when I was at Enrique's parents' house that I decided I needed to lose weight. I looked in the mirror and hated what I saw. As a result, I came up with a novel idea: I would just stop eating. I went for days without eating anything more than a bowl of soup or some other insignificant amount of food, and I did manage to lose weight, albeit through a very unhealthy route.

Because I was not eating, I stopped producing milk and it was when Aaron was six weeks old that I was forced to put him on the bottle. I felt guilty about not being able to give nourishment to my child, but I simply could not produce enough milk to satisfy him.

At no time did Enrique ever speak to me about the fact that I was not eating. I suppose he had his own demons to contend with, which were in all probability much worse than my eating disorder, so if he noticed that I wasn't eating, I doubt he cared.

On the evening before we were supposed to fly to Little Rock to see my family, I woke up in the middle of the night to feed and change Aaron. Enrique woke up as well, quite uncharacteristically, and said something that I do not now recall.

I replied rather sarcastically to Enrique's comment, probably because I was exhausted and tired of his behaviour. As soon as the words came out of my mouth, Enrique sat up and began hitting me with the full force of his fists. To protect myself, I shielded myself from his blows with the pillow on the bed. After Enrique vented his rage on me, he laid back down and went right back to sleep, content in the knowledge that he had once again assaulted his wife while his child lay in the cot beside her.

I don't suppose Enrique gave a thought in the world about the values and morals he was instilling in his son. If anything, I suppose Enrique felt quite justified in physically and mentally abusing me and would therefore endeavour to teach his son to do the same.

The following day, while we sat in the airport, waiting to fly to Little Rock, Enrique apologised to me for hitting me. I made no comment. There was simply nothing I could say. What do you say to your husband and the father of your child, the person who you were actually once in love with, after he has just attacked you in a most viscous and brutal manner? Nothing.

Although Enrique had not come near me in a sexual manner in the past year, suddenly when we were in Arkansas he wanted to have sex. When we were in the downstairs bedroom, he put his hands around my waist and started kissing me. I recoiled in horror. Enrique had found it difficult even to be civil to me during the previous year, and now he was trying to kiss me.

Being a typical male. Enrique was only nice to me when he wanted to have intercourse. What I would like to know is, in view of his high sex drive, if he were not sleeping with me for the previous year, whom was he sleeping with?

The following morning Enrique woke me up at 5:00am for sex. I was reluctant because of the pain and the possibility of getting pregnant again. Enrique told me not to worry because he did not mind if we had another baby. But what about me? What if I minded? Didn't I have a say as to whether or not I had another baby? The first was bad enough!

Even though the thought of engaging in an intimate physical act with a man who had been so hateful to me for such a long time made me physically ill, I acquiesced and gave my husband what he wanted. Only a survivor of child abuse could endure such a situation.

It was also in Little Rock that Enrique told me that he had a boil on his bottom and wanted to see a doctor. It was a reasonable request but I did not know what to do. Throughout my whole childhood, I had only seen a doctor once. Although my mother used her day off, Tuesday, as her day to make the never-ending round to see an assortment of specialists about her various physical ailments, I was left to fend for myself. It was only by the grace of God that I survived my childhood and became an adult because whenever I became ill, my mother just left me to die and I suppose she thought I survived just to spite her. Because I did not know any doctors in Little Rock, I told my mother Enrique wanted to see one. When he realised that I clearly did not know what to do, he said it was okay and he really didn't want to see a doctor anyway.

Enrique's need for total control extended to my mother as well. He was very unhappy about the way she was holding Aaron. I looked and everything seemed fine but on a second look I noticed that his outfit was pulling at his leg. I therefore adjusted outfit to make him more comfortable. By trying to govern every single event in Aaron's life, not only did Enrique make me feel inadequate, but my mother as well.

From my mother's house, we drove to Tyndall Air Force Base, Florida, just outside Panama City. I was going to be working at Cape San Blas, which was 38 miles away, just two miles short of a remote. Enrique and I stayed at the BAQ while I in-processed and found a place to live. It was while I was in-processing that I was to discover that Enrique had registered Aaron as his dependent, and not mine, and that he therefore received all of the money for Aaron. Although I was quite annoyed, I was not surprised that Enrique would do something like that. He would go on to do a great deal more to usurp my authority as a wife and mother.

While we were staying in the BAQ, Enrique got his sex drive back. He wanted sex every day and he did not care whether Aaron was in the room with us or not when he took what he considered to be his conjugal rights.

The thought of having sex literally turned my stomach but I did not want to upset Enrique. I therefore put my own wants, needs and desires to the side and did my duty. It upset me; however, that Enrique was quite happy to engage in sexual intercourse with me when Aaron was in the same room, sometimes wide awake.

It's funny, really, that Enrique constantly tried to take the moral high ground and act as if he were somehow more pure or chaste than me. My question is this: how can a man consider himself moral when he sexually takes his wife while his young son is in the same room? The fact is that Enrique was righteous only when it suited him to be so. The rest of the time he was just like any other sex-crazed maniac. I think it is more appropriate to say that Enrique was not righteous, but self-righteous.

Within a week, I found a one-bedroom bungalow for us to live in between Mexico Beach and Cape San Blas. One unusual aspect was that I lived in the central time zone and worked in the eastern time zone.

Wherever we lived, I was expected to pay all of the bills and do everything that needed to be done to enable us to live safely and comfortably. I was responsible for cleaning the house, fixing all of the meals, taking care of Aaron, working full time, and making sure that all of the bills were paid. Enrique was responsible for... well... not much of anything, really. Is it any wonder that I was exhausted and on the verge of collapse most of the time?

I was not happy about the domestic situation at all. Never in my wildest dreams did I imagine I would marry a good for nothing bum who lay back and took it easy while I slaved away to bring the bacon home and then cook it too.

I asked Enrique on several occasions to go out and get a job, and every time he refused. The excuse he gave was that he had to look after Aaron, but that was not true. I looked after Aaron. I prepared his meals, washed him, fed him, played with him, and got up with him in the middle of the night or early in the morning when he woke up. Enrique didn't look after Aaron, he was just there.

Enrique would get up when Aaron made him get up. He would wander into the living room and watch television or read a book. He never played with Aaron or talked to him, but just left him in his rocker or playpen all day long. To be honest, Aaron would have been better off in a day-care centre because at least then he would have had some mental stimulation and learned valuable social skills. Enrique would not have any of that, however, because if Aaron was in a day-care centre, he would have to go out and get a job.

Not long after we moved into our little one bedroom bungalow, Enrique's father came to visit. He flew to Florida from Puerto Rico, where he spent most of his time. When Enrique's father arrived, I became very agitated because he drank Heineken beer. There was no rational explanation whatsoever because Enrique's father had never been anything other than nice to me. I can only assume that although I have no conscious recall of any such event, I must have been very frightened and subjected to abuse when adults around me drank. Although I no doubt blanked any memories from my mind, I have always instinctively been very wary of people who drink.

Enrique and I never kept any alcohol in the house because we did not drink on a regular basis. On the one occasion when Enrique came home drunk, after a night out with colleagues, I became very upset and let him know in no uncertain terms that I did not approve of that kind of behaviour.

Enrique never discussed with me his decision to leave the Air Force. It was his choice and I did not have a say in the matter. While he was in the military, he wrote letters to his friends and family, telling them that he could not wait to get out of the Air Force, which he called the 'Air Farce'.

For someone who hated the Air Force so much, he made a model airman. He maintained impeccable standards of dress and appearance, and would spend hours polishing his shoes. I, on the other hand, had a rather slapdash attitude to my appearance. I gave my uniforms a lick and a promise, and did not particularly care how I looked.

During the final commander's call, Enrique was asked to say something about his impending departure from the squadron and the Air Force. He stood up in front of everyone who was there and gave a long speech, which he may or may not have prepared in advance. I barely listened to what he said, but the basic gist of it was that he could not wait to get out of the Air Force because he really hated it.

Enrique then did a really odd thing by taking Aaron and displaying him to the crowd, saying that his son was the most important thing to him. Although Aaron was only a few weeks old he was already Enrique's trophy. Perhaps Enrique wanted to have Aaron around to prove that he really could sire a child, I will never know.

Because Enrique, by his own admission, hated the Air Force so much, I would have thought he would have been happy to see the back of it. That was not the case, however, as he never hesitated to remind me of my military duties.

Enrique paid with his own money to have a photograph taken of him in his military uniform. He then made a plaque composed of an assortment of regalia, such as stripes, ribbons and other ornaments that he had collected during his five years in the military.

What struck me as particularly odd was the fact that for someone who really hated the Air Force and could not wait to get out, Enrique was certainly living in the past. He did not want to go out and get a job and create his own destiny, but preferred instead to reminisce about his past military experiences, a time when he must have felt he was somebody special.

While Enrique was living a life of leisure and I was working my fingers to the bone both at work and at home, my eating disorder became progressively worse. I lived in a state of virtual starvation, yet could not get lower than 130 pounds no matter how hard I tried.

For breakfast I would have puffed rice and milk. For lunch I would have a salad with tuna, and I would go home and prepare a reasonable dinner. At the weekends, I would endeavour to eat nothing at all, but quite often succumbed to my sweet tooth and would have cookies or cake.

Considering the little amount of food I was eating, one would have thought I would be rail thin. That was not the case, however, because my metabolism is so slow that I could live on nothing but water for an indefinite period. Any normal person would have simply withered away, but not me. No matter how hard I tried, the pounds would simply not go away.

I suppose I should be grateful that I have been blessed/cursed with a metabolism that runs along at a snail's pace. If it were not for the fact that I can live on a very low calorie diet for a really long time, I would never have survived my first couple of years of life because my mother did not see feeding me or my siblings as a priority.

I should be grateful that I survived a childhood in which any normal child might well have starved to death; I should be pleased that I lived to tell the tale, but I am not happy at all about it. As far as I am concerned, I had nothing to live for and would have been better off dead. Some power much greater than me, however, decided otherwise, so who am I to complain about the fact that I was spared a slow, withering expiry. Who am I to dispute the fact that I was sent down to Earth to endure a horrendous childhood and maturation only so I could suffer chronic depression every single day of my miserable, pathetic life. I suppose the only good thing to come out of what I consider to be a total sham of a life is that I could write a book about my experiences, hoping that others will learn from them.

It was while I was living in the bungalow that I decided to write my friend, Sherry, a letter. I was very unhappy because I had written her repeatedly and had not received a reply. In the letter, I told her that I was very angry with her for not writing me back and I ended the letter by telling her that I had always been a friend to her.

A couple of weeks later I received a telephone call from Sherry at my work. We talked for a while and I thought the conversation went well. I promptly went home and wrote her another letter, but never heard from her again.

At that time I was too young and naïve to realise that people are very fickle beings and befriend others for a variety of reasons. I had not yet realised that people come and go from our lives as it suits them. As we grow and evolve along our Earth walk, we come into contact with those individuals who will help us to achieve our goals at varying times in our lives. It is for that reason that friendship is for the most part a very transient phenomenon.

Instead of being hurt that Sherry was no longer interested in friendship with me, I should have taken it all in stride and accepted her rejection gracefully. I would have a long way to go before I could rationally accept a person did not want to be a part of my life.

Because I was living in a state of exhaustion, working endlessly at work and at home, my health was the first thing to suffer. I had never been given an opportunity to recover from a very difficult pregnancy and a traumatic labour and delivery. No sooner had I experienced all of that than I was thrown into a situation in which I was working 18 hours a day and was subjected to constant sleep deprivation.

I never even got to sleep in at the weekends because Enrique decided that he needed a break from lounging around the house all week long and would stay in bed while Aaron cried for attention. I therefore would be required to get up and go downstairs and play with my son while my layabout husband slept in bed upstairs.

Because I never had any respite from my responsibilities, I was sick all the time. At least once a month I would have to go to the emergency room at the hospital on Tyndall Air Force Base with some mystery illness. I would usually have a fever and an infection, and the doctor would prescribe me antibiotics to kill the bacterial infection that invaded my body.

One day I was bitten on the left index finger by a spider. The wound became severely infected and again I developed a fever. Eventually a huge ball of puss was dislodged from my finger, and to this day I sport a nasty scar as a remembrance of the time when my body's immune system could not even tackle a spider bite.

I suppose that although I did not consciously recognise the fact that I had been malnourished as a child, the memory must have stayed with me on a primordial level. Therefore, every time

Aaron cried I would give him a bottle. To my way of thinking, feeding my child was an act of love. I fed my son because I had not been fed as a baby. I nourished my child because I had not been nourished. I knew I fed Aaron too much, but I didn't care. I wanted to give him all the love that I was never given as a child. I loved my son very much.

After we had lived in the little one-bedroom bungalow for about six months, Enrique decided that he wanted to move. He selected a two-bedroom town house in Mexico Beach that seemed nice enough. The rent was more, but Enrique was not concerned in the least about the bills because he did not pay them. Therefore, one October day my colleagues helped me to move our belongings to our new accommodation.

The one thing Enrique did do was to make sure Aaron slept in the spare bedroom. When Aaron was safely asleep in his crib, Enrique would want to have sex with me. Because Enrique had no responsibilities whatsoever, he had all the time in the world to cultivate his sex drive and fantasise about having sex with me or anybody else while his son was asleep in the other room.

I, on the other hand, recoiled in horror. I was exhausted all the time and deeply resented Enrique for the way he treated me and the fact that he put the responsibility of providing for the family all on my shoulders. I had always wanted a strong man who provided for his family, and instead I was stuck with a good for nothing bum who kicked back and took it easy while I worked myself into a state of physical, and then eventually mental, illness. The thought of sex with Enrique turned my stomach. Every time he touched me, I was physically ill.

Enrique just viewed me as his personal meal ticket and sex slave, so he was not happy at all with my reluctance to serve as vehicle for his physical relief. There was one such occasion when Enrique asked me, 'Do you want to have sex?'

I justifiably told him that I was tired and wanted to sleep. Enrique became enraged and retorted, 'What do you want? Do you just want to have sex once a week?' before he stormed out of the bedroom and went downstairs to watch the *David Letterman Show.*

I was relieved that I did not have to have sex, but upset by Enrique's attitude. If he had to get up early every morning to go to work, come home and fix dinner, spend the evening looking after his child, and then get up in the middle of the night and early in the morning to take care of his child, he would not be feeling very romantic either. Instead, Enrique did sweet fuck-all and expected me to lie on my back and spread my legs so he could get some sexual satisfaction. I don't think so.

To be honest, the thought of having sex with Enrique made me sick to my stomach. I tried to have sex with him as little as possible, and considered myself lucky if I only had to do it once a week. I was constantly anxious about it.

One thing that totally repulsed me was the fact that Enrique would masturbate himself while he was lying in bed with me. It was a little difficult to ignore, because I could sense him jerking his hand back and forth while he was in bed with me. I did not say anything about it, but I found it to be a total turn off. If Enrique had to do that sort of thing, I wished he didn't do it around me. What he saw as a perfectly normal function I viewed with disgust.

The people I worked with did not have a high regard for Enrique because they thought that he should be out earning a living, providing for his family. They would have really been shocked if they knew that Enrique adamantly refused to get a job and sat around the house all day long, doing nothing except reading books and watching television. My colleagues didn't know, because I didn't tell them, that I was not only the bread-winner but was responsible for making sure that all of the house-hold duties were taken care of as well.

Enrique never lifted a finger to help me, yet he could not understand why I was angry with him most of the time. He thought his behaviour was perfectly acceptable. He was only doing what his own father had done and nobody, except maybe his mother, had raised any objections to that. Enrique's own father had given up work years earlier, leaving his mother to pay all of the bills, provide for the family, and make sure the house was maintained as well. Enrique knew very well how much his father's behaviour upset his mother, but such awareness never stopped him from following in his father's footsteps. Because his father was a man of leisure, Enrique must have felt that he too deserved that lifestyle.

With such an unsupportive home life, is it any wonder I was depressed? Against my better judgement, I went to the mental health clinic on base. The first thing they did was to give me a test to make sure that I wasn't crazy. After they felt safe in the knowledge that they did not have a psychopath in their midst, they told me that I could attend a group therapy session based on single people, which took place every fortnight. I thought it was quite odd that they should class me with single people because I was married with a child, but for some reason they thought that I was better suited in that environment.

On one of my fortnightly visits to my singles group therapy session, I mentioned that whenever Enrique became angry I would go around the house hiding sharp objects. At that point in our relationship I still believed Enrique would not do anything to intentionally harm me, but in the throes of his rage I was afraid that I might inadvertently be a casualty while he was throwing things and swinging his fists. Because I had been raised in a home where violence and abuse were perfectly acceptable behaviour, I did not see any cause for concern about the fact that I had to hide the sharp objects in the house. I just thought it made common sense.

The psychologists running the group therapy session had other ideas. They thought it was appalling that I had to live in a state of terror. Sadly, although I was only 23, that was the first time in my life when anyone, bar my paternal grandmother, ever expressed any concern for my welfare. I had been passed from pillar to post for so many years that my own wants and needs were never taken into consideration. I was always expected to go along with what everybody else wanted.

Having been brought up in a Baptist family, when a colleague invited me to the Baptist church in Mexico Beach, I made it a habit to go every Sunday. I tried to be religious even though I had never had particularly good experiences with religious people. Because I didn't know anybody in the area, I would sit on my own and would not stay to socialise with people after the service was over.

Enrique would rarely, if ever, go to church with me. He was not a particularly religious person when I met him, but strangely, he began reading the Bible shortly after Aaron was born. The odd thing was that Enrique was reading the Bible and interpreting it on his own. He did not have a support network to help him make sense of those ancient texts that were, although inspired by God, still written by men and therefore still fallible. History is full of religious fanatics who have interpreted the Bible to suit their own needs; such as Jim Jones and his cult in Guyana, David Koresh and the Branch Davidians, both of which ended in disaster, and Charles Manson and his family.

It is important to note that 45 per cent of mental illnesses have a religious element. That is not to say that religion makes people crazy, but merely that mentally ill people are naturally predisposed to religion in their quest for illumination in a mental fog of disarray. I do not know, therefore, if Enrique had a psychotic experience with religious overtones, which caused him to want to read the Bible. I do know, though, that he repeatedly told me he needed to get his head sorted out and he thought he was going to go crazy. Enrique was becoming totally immersed in the Bible, although he did not adopt any particular religious path. One day I suggested that he should read a book written by Dr Joyce Brothers, a famous American psychologist. Enrique looked up and piously informed me, 'The Bible is all I need.'

Well, what could I say to that? Not much.

If a person were to read four chapters of the Bible every day, he would have read it from cover to cover in a year. I never managed to read the Bible through in one go, but I did read it every night and reflect upon its contents. After reading my Bible, I would pray to the Lord in Heaven and ask him to help me to be a good wife and mother. I was so very deeply unhappy. I did everything I was supposed to do to be a good Christian, but I was still miserable. I believed in God and Jesus with all my heart, but why was I so sad?

Even though I prayed to God every single day, I don't think he heard my prayers. If he did, he had a rather sick sense of humour. I had never done anything to anybody in my life, and I certainly did not deserve to have to work so hard and have such a terrible man for a husband.

If Enrique did pray to God, I doubt seriously that he ever asked God to help him to be a good husband and father. If he did make such a request, I don't suppose God listened to him, either. If he did, he really must have had a demented sense of humour. Good husbands and fathers provide for their families, not lie around the house all day long.

Enrique decided that for the New Year we would go to Lawrence, Massachusetts, to see his family. He was going whether I went or not, so I decided to go along. Enrique bought his ticket and I bought mine. It did not go unnoticed that while Enrique did not have any money to help out with the bills, he did have money for himself. He did not, I would like to stress, have any money for my ticket, the woman who had been keeping him for the past year.

I suppose that trip to Lawrence was quite prophetic, really. Of all of the photographs taken, not one of them had me in them. I can only assume that it was the universe's way of removing me from that family, little by little.

When I came back to work after having spent the New Year in

Lawrence, I was quite surprised to learn that I had been given an assignment to Germany. To be honest, I did not even know where Germany was, I was that unsophisticated. To be fair, however, most Americans are so insular and self-obsessed that they are doing well just to know the names of the two countries bordering their own. Expecting the typical American to have any awareness of a country that is an ocean and a continent away is asking a bit much, I am afraid.

I was to be assigned to the 602nd Tactical Control Squadron in Neu Ulm, Germany. I did not know what a tactical unit did, but I would soon find out. When I arrived at my assignment, I would discover that my job would be to go out and play war games several times a year.

Before I could go to Germany, however, I would have to go back to Keesler Air Force Base, Mississippi, and attend an AN/TRC-97A radio course. Not to become too technical, the TRC-97, as it was fondly called, was a radio set that had 24 multiplex channels connected to a radio. The radio set was a fixed line of sight radio that could transmit anywhere from 1 watt to a kilowatt at a frequency range of 4.4 to 5 Gigahertz. It could be connected to one of three antennas, depending on the distance and signal needed. These antennas had to be constructed, so knowledge of mechanics as well as electronics was needed to work on that equipment.

The TRC-97 was initially made for the Marine Corps and originally only had 12 channels, but when the Air Force decided to use it they added an additional 12 channels in another module called the Baby Mux. Under the care of the Marines, the radio set was expected to last three months, but when the Air Force took over that versatile signalling device, they had been using it for more than 20 years!

The humble frequency modulated radio set would eventually be superseded by a more modern digital version called the AN/TRC-170, but the old FM radio proved its worth time after time, far exceeding its original three-month life expectancy as predicted by the Marine Corps.

I asked the Air Force if I could go directly to my assignment to Germany when I finished my AN/TRC-97 training course and was refused. As a result, I would be required to go to the course in May, return in July, and then leave for Germany at the end of August. I was not happy about the situation, but considering the fact that the Air Force owned me body and soul, there was not much I could do about it. To further complicate the matter, my family would not be allowed to go to Germany with me. I would have to travel on my own, go on a waiting list just to be allowed to look for a house, and then, when I found a property, send for my family. The military's philosophy was, famously, that if they wanted me to have a family, they would have issued me one. I was so brainwashed into the military way of thinking that it never occurred to me that I might be just as deserving of a family as anybody else.

It is funny, really, that America considers itself to be such a progressive nation when, socially, it actually lags behind Europe by decades. For example, America still has the barbaric death penalty. Anyone who supports the death penalty should ask himself, 'Why do we kill people to show people that killing people is wrong?'

The European Union has a Human Rights Act, 1998, which details basic human rights that everybody should be entitled to. America proclaims to the world what a great country it is, but as far as I am aware it does not have an equivalent to Europe's Human Rights Act.

In fact, America often violates people's human rights, as evidenced by their treatment of the al Qaeda suspects who have been held at Camp X-Ray, Guantanamo Bay, Cuba. Two hundred days after the al Qaeda suspects were flown to Camp X-Ray, they still had not been charged with any offences.

The al Qaeda suspects were flown shackled and hooded to

Camp X-Ray. None of them was allowed legal representation despite the power of military tribunals to order the death penalty. Amnesty International became involved and said, 'The more cells Mr Bush adds at Guantanamo Bay, the more America's reputation as a defender of international justice will suffer.'

If America will abuse people's human rights by maintaining the barbaric and inhumane death penalty and abusing suspects at Camp X-ray, one could scarcely expect them to flinch at the prospect of separating me from my son. Unfortunately, at that time I had no idea just how insignificant I was to the American government. They saw me as cannon fodder and nothing more. It is such a shame that I did not realise that sad fact sooner.

Living a life of leisure did nothing to improve Enrique's disposition. He was just as nasty, lazy and self-serving as ever. He still continued with his sleep deprivation techniques because sleep was the one thing I never got enough of. Sometimes he would wake me up after I had collapsed from exhaustion and would start yelling at me about one thing or another. I can remember his standing over me, staring at me with a hateful grimace on his face, ranting and raving over some real or imagined wrong I had committed. On one occasion he even took a cake I had made and threw it in the trash.

Even though Enrique could do pretty much what he wanted all day, every day, he still insisted on his own free time. He would take college courses, which meant that he was away from home one night a week. On one occasion, he actually suggested that I should take a college course. I looked at him in amazement. When, I asked him, would I have time to take a college course? I was either working or busy at home taking care of Aaron. I knew that Enrique would not allow me the free time necessary to complete the course work required and told him so. He did not respond to my rather angry accusation because he knew it was true. He only looked after Aaron while I was working; it was my responsibility to look after him the rest of the time.

Enrique also liked to go to the movies, so quite often he would leave me at home to look after Aaron while he went to the cinema. I never begrudged him living his own life, taking college courses, and going to the movies, because I was so shattered that most of the time I simply did not want to do the things most people my age were doing.

One night when Enrique was off to the movies, I collapsed in exhaustion. Normally going to sleep would have been quite okay, but Aaron was wide awake and wanted to explore the world. I knew I should stay up with him, but having to work full time and look after Aaron for the past year had taken its toll on my fragile body. A body could only take so much, and mine decided it needed rest. I therefore took Aaron into my bedroom and he amused himself by crawling around. My mind wanted so badly to get out of bed and take care of my baby, but my body would not respond. I simply could not move and I could not open my eyes. I was so terribly worried about Aaron's welfare and fortunately he did not get into any harm. I would have been too weak to do anything about it if he had.

I doubt very seriously that Enrique gave any consideration at all to the fact that his refusal to contribute to the family finances or help out in the house was destroying me body and soul. I doubt very seriously that if he had known just how much he was hurting me that he would have cared. Like most men, Enrique thought that as long as he was okay, that was all that mattered. I married a really nice man – not.

One time when Enrique and I were shopping in the Base Exchange, he asked me to get my pocketbook out of my shoulder bag. I rummaged around my bag and was alarmed to find it missing. Enrique looked at me derisively and handed it back to me. He had stolen it from me. He said he did it to prove a point because I should have been watching my handbag. The fact that I had my hands full with Aaron was beside the point. It occurred to me that he was becoming a rather nasty person.

It was Aaron's first birthday. He had been up all day, going to the park and shopping, and naturally he only wanted to go to sleep. Enrique, however, wanted a party. I made a cake, but it was not ready until late in the evening. By this time Aaron was very tired and clearly wanted to go to bed. Enrique kept poking him and prodding him, making him eat cake that he was clearly too tired to enjoy. Finally, Aaron broke down in tears and began to howl. He was tired and wanted to go to bed. I felt very sorry for my son because I knew exactly what it was like to be exhausted and want nothing more than to go to bed. Enrique had deprived me of sleep many times before. Our whole lives revolved around Enrique and what he wanted. No one else's needs mattered, and Aaron was no exception. Enrique would force Aaron to do whatever he wanted in the same way that he forced me.

During Aaron's party, I was speaking to Enrique about something when he interrupted me. I was tired and asked him not to interrupt me before finishing my train of thought. Enrique was incensed that I should dare to tell him not to interrupt me and I could see the rage welling up inside him. I was so tired that I really didn't care, and went to bed collapsing in a heap on the bed.

While I slept, Enrique had plenty of time to go over in his mind how I could dare to ask him not to interrupt me, and at about 10:30 he could contain his rage no longer. He woke me up with the same familiar tirade that I had heard a hundred times before. For the first time though, something inside of me had changed. Enrique could say or do whatever he liked because I simply did not care any more. Enrique no longer had any effect on me at all.

As Enrique stood by the bed, I told him quite honestly that I didn't care any more. I didn't love him any more, and I was tired of him waking me up in the middle of the night, yelling and screaming at me.

You could have knocked Enrique over with a feather. He was

totally shocked. He honestly believed that he could behave like a brute day in and day out for years on end and that I would continue to love him. He was in such a state of total disbelief that he left the room.

The following morning, Enrique skulked around the room like a naughty little school boy. He knew that he had gone too far because his demeanour clearly reflected this. Like any abusive man, Enrique apologetically told me that he loved me, but as far as I was concerned, it was just words. If he loved me he would have contributed to the family and helped me around the house. Enrique did not have a clue in the world what love was. Within several months of Aaron's birth, I had realised that Enrique had taken over complete control of every aspect of Aaron's life. It saddened me because Enrique did not even want Aaron, but as soon as he was born he did a complete about face. Aaron was supposed to be my baby, but Enrique had taken him from me body and soul. Enrique did not see me as a wife and mother but as some slave, who would go to work and earn money, and then come home, clean the house, and service him sexually to boot.

I was very disappointed at how my whole domestic situation had turned out in a way that I had never envisaged. Through my deep depression, I would often find myself saying, 'The next baby I have will be mine.'

On only one occasion did Aaron ever cry out for me specifically. Enrique and I had gone shopping at the Base Exchange, and Enrique took Aaron, as usual. As I began to walk away, Aaron held his hands out to me and began crying. I thought it was so sweet that Aaron wanted his mother. Unfortunately that was the only time that I am aware of that he ever called out for me.

Because I had been pushed to the end of my tether, when Enrique and I had arguments I would lash out at him. I would tell Enrique over and over to go back to Boston. I really didn't want him with me any more because he contributed absolutely nothing to the relationship, financially or emotionally. The only thing that

Enrique did was to watch Aaron while I was at work and that was all. I did absolutely everything else, and I could not carry on that way any longer.

Keesler

I took the Greyhound Bus from Panama City, Florida, to Biloxi, Mississipi, and was met by John, Enrique's friend from the Azores. John had been given a special duty assignment to Keesler and would be working as a technical instructor when he finished his training. It was nice to have a friend at Keesler, a place where I knew nobody.

John took me to the dormitory where I would be staying for the next five weeks. I would be sharing a room with another person, which was a surreal situation indeed. I definitely was not happy with my first roommate because she would allow her boyfriend to sleep with her in the room. I found it to be an uncomfortable situation to say the very least.

I decided that since I would have a lot of time on my hands, I would take up jogging. There was a scenic track on the base that I could use, so every day after school, I would run six laps, which amounted to a mile and a half. I didn't realise it at the time, but for the first time in a year I wasn't totally exhausted. For the first time in I don't know how long, I could do whatever I wanted to do.

Enrique came to Keesler after I had been there a couple of weeks. The plan was that he would visit me and then drive to Little Rock to spend some time with my family. That was the plan, anyway; Enrique always did exactly what he wanted to do with little regard for anybody else.

On the day Enrique arrived, we went to a party at John's house. I can only suppose that Enrique loved being with John again because he seemed much more interested in his friend than in me. By about 10:00, I was shattered and wanted to go home. I told Enrique that I would take Aaron back to the room we had rented. When I got there, I settled Aaron into bed and went to bed myself, collapsing from exhaustion.

In the middle of the night, I woke up to find my husband on top of me, relieving his sexual urges. Enrique never asked my consent. He just took what he considered to be his conjugal rights. He also made sure that I was sleeping when he did it because he did not want me to make a fuss. Now honestly, what kind of a man waits until a woman is asleep before he has sex with her?

Extensive studies into male behaviour have proved beyond any doubt that the vast majority of men only get married for sex or money, or both. Enrique, therefore, must have thought that Christmas had come early when he met me because he got both sex and money without having to treat me with even an ounce of respect.

On the Sunday, we decided to go to my room. Enrique promptly made himself at home on my bed and took a nap. Because I was tired, as usual, I lay down on the floor and dozed off into a fitful slumber. My health was so fragile that the mere act of sleeping on the cold floor was all I needed to propel me into yet another illness. Therefore, within 24 hours I already had chills and the flu-like symptoms that I had become so accustomed to.

There was no possibility for me to phone in sick, which is what anyone in a civilian job would be allowed to do. The military, however, takes a dim view of malingering, so people are forced to go to work even when they are unwell. Therefore, I somehow managed to attend my training course and look after Aaron even though I was extremely ill.

Enrique decided to throw a tantrum on the day he was supposed to leave to go back to Florida. We had arranged to meet at my 10:00 break, so when we were released from class I went to the lady's room and then looked for Enrique and Aaron whilst speaking to a colleague as I walked down the hall.

Enrique must have been incensed to see me enjoying myself and speaking to someone, so the minute he saw me he started yelling at me and made a scene in front of everyone in the building.

I tried to explain to Enrique that I had to use the toilet during my break, but it was no good. He, having been in the military himself, knew very well that I could not just get up and leave whenever I wanted, so I was understandably perplexed by his behaviour.

I went to give Aaron a hug and a kiss before he left, but Enrique yanked him from me before I could say farewell to my son. I suppose even then Enrique knew he could use Aaron to hurt me, which goes a long way to describe exactly how his mind works. I was very hurt by what Enrique had done, but I repressed my feelings. Having endured an abusive childhood and subsequent marriage, I had learned a long time ago to survive austere circumstances.

Within a couple of days of Enrique's leaving, I developed a boil on my labia majora, which was quite painful because I had a great deal of difficulty sitting, walking, or doing just about anything. It is interesting to note that when I was with Enrique I was always coming down with illnesses, and many of them were sexual in nature. He initially passed on urinary tract infections to me and this had progressed to boils. Enrique had also rubbed me raw on one occasion and I was in so much agony that I had a great deal of difficulty walking. In addition, I would suffer flu-like symptoms almost on a monthly basis. Thanks to Enrique, my health had gone to Hell in a hand basket.

Because I was in so much pain, I made an appointment to see a doctor that afternoon. The appointment interfered with my course, and I was therefore obliged to tell my instructor that I had to leave early to see a doctor. From the look on his face, it was obvious he was not happy that I had to leave early. Although he did not say I could not go, I was unnerved nonetheless. Whilst at the doctor, I was prescribed antibiotics, which seemed to clear up the problem.

It was also around the time that I was plagued with the boil that I succumbed to yet another urinary tract infection. That too was just one more consequence of having sexual intercourse with Enrique. I have no idea why I had so many health problems since marrying him. Maybe one day he will be able to shed a little light on that mystery for me.

One evening when I was standing in the foyer of the dormitory a tall, young, good-looking man approached me and began a conversation. I was so naïve that I had no idea this man was trying to chat me up, so I innocently kept up the banter. To be honest, I had been rejected, humiliated, and degraded by my husband so much that I was not aware of the fact that many men saw me as attractive. As Sarah Ferguson, the Duchess of York, would say, I was an affair waiting to happen.

It was during this presumably innocent conversation that Patrick asked me if I would help him with his coursework. He was attending the basic electronic course and told me that he was having difficulties calculating peak, peak to peak, and average voltage. I loved electronics and was quite happy to help him with the areas that he told me he was having difficulties with.

I have to say that I was so naïve and considered myself to be so unattractive that I really believed he needed help with his studies. Anyone more streetwise, however, would have been able to spot his chat-up line a mile away.

We set a day and time for me to go to Patrick's room and help him with his studies. I went to his room and had a thoroughly enjoyable time. It was one of the first times in an extremely long time that anyone paid any attention to me at all. I left Patrick's room floating on air. He took an interest in me, which is something that so rarely occurred in my life. I must say that the only interest that Enrique ever took of me was when he wanted me to pay the bills, clean the house, or operate as a vehicle to allow him to release his sexual urges.

Patrick agreed to go running with me, which I thought was a very nice thing to do. Once we were on the track, however, it was clear that the running arrangement was clearly not going to work out. My running partner was almost a foot taller than me, and being much healthier, he was naturally swifter.

Patrick also took me to the movies at the mall in Biloxi. It seemed that within a very short time, we were spending a great deal of time with each other. I did not realise it, but the attention he paid to me made me really like him a lot.

I suppose that I did feel a bit guilty about spending time with a man who was not my husband, so I decided to give Enrique one last chance to redeem himself.

I phoned him and began a rather innocuous conversation, just to see how it would go. I then made sure that I threw in one important question.

'Do you miss me?' I asked my husband.

'No...!' Enrique sneered back.

That was all I needed to know. In our entire relationship I had never made any demands whatsoever on Enrique. He pretty much did as he pleased and I organised my life around him. In 4½ years, I had never asked Enrique for a thing. All I wanted to know was if he had missed me, and through his own admission, he didn't.

If Enrique did not miss me then, as far as I was concerned, I could do pretty much what I wanted. Relationships are about mutual love, respect and trust, and that is something I had never experienced with Enrique, or any other man for that matter.

Because Enrique treated me with complete disregard and contempt, I did not see any reason why I should not spend time with Patrick, since he obviously was interested in me. I therefore agreed to go to the NCO Club with Patrick for dinner. I must say that was one of the first times that a man had ever taken me to dinner. Most of the men I went out with always behaved as if I should be grateful they were taking me out.

I was so nervous about going out with Patrick that I literally could not eat. I had lost my appetite from the excitement of what I was doing. It was that evening that I went to bed with Patrick. I really could not believe it was all happening; it was such a surreal experience. I felt very guilty about what I had done, but it was too late. I already knew that I was an adultress. I was destined to burn in Hell for my sin. The scarlet letter had been indelibly marked on my forehead. During my infatuation, I wrote Patrick a love letter, telling him that he was my knight in shining armour. When I gave him the letter, he did not seem to be overly impressed with it. I did not realise it because I did not have enough experience to know, but Patrick was bored already. For him, as with most men, the thrill was in the chase and conquest. After he got what he wanted, which was me, he was not interested any more. Just like a wild animal, Patrick did not want to maintain a lasting relationship. The chase was what motivated him to take any interest in me at all. It is such a shame that I was not more streetwise and astute to the ways of wild men.

It happened that my affair with Patrick began at the very end of my time at Keesler, so it lasted for a grand total of three days. For me, it was short and very, very intense.

As I was preparing to leave Keesler, I went to see John at his home. I related to him that I had met someone and John told me that he did not want to hear it. John was really Enrique's friend and not mine, and he justifiably did not want to get involved in my love life. John was not entirely unsympathetic, however, because he invited me over to his home on my 23rd birthday when I was seven months pregnant, when Enrique abandoned me to go on holiday to Spain. Although John never said anything about his friend's erratic behaviour, he certainly could not have been pleased about it.

John also told me that he could understand why I would want to leave Enrique because he knew something was definitely not right in his head. John took particular offence at the fact that during Enrique's final commander's call, instead of saying farewell gracefully, he stood up and gave a long-winded speech and basically told everyone to fuck off. Needless to say, Enrique must have offended a lot of people when he gave that speech. I personally don't recall exactly what he said because I was still zonked out from giving birth.

My course finished on 3rd July but I decided to spend one last day with Patrick. I felt very guilty about what I had done and told him so. He was not particularly bothered about my feelings that I had sinned because his motivation was primarily sexual in nature. In retrospect, I suppose I was just one of many women who Patrick had bedded when he was away from home.

Patrick was not concerned in the least that he had torn my emotions apart. To him, a typical womaniser, I was not a person with feelings and emotions, but just another conquest. Once he had me, he did not want me any more.

It was also one day I spent with Patrick that I noticed a duality to his personality. He seemed to be very paranoid that someone was going to steal his credit cards. While he told me quite clearly he did not like black people, he went out of his way to make conversation with them and even went so far as to change his way of speaking to sound more black. For Patrick it was all just a game. Because I was so naïve and inexperienced, I had no idea how insincere he really was.

On 5th July, the day that I left Keesler, Patrick agreed to say goodbye to me before he left. When he arrived, I could tell that he was clearly preoccupied. He seemed to be more concerned about how he looked in his uniform than saying goodbye to me.

I was unhappy to say goodbye to Patrick. It seemed like we had only just got together and now we had to part. Perhaps that was the appeal for Patrick. He knew I would be leaving before he had an opportunity to become bored.

I took the bus back to Panama City and cried the whole way home.

Breaking Up Is Easy To Do

On Friday, 5th July 1984, Enrique picked me up from the bus station. Needless to say, I was not very happy. If Enrique noticed, he never said anything. That was nothing unusual, however, because he never ever enquired about my welfare. He seemed to have no interest in how anybody else might be feeling.

That evening I sent him to the movies. He was quite happy to go out and did not appear to want to spend any time with me at all. I spent the evening writing letters to Patrick, but did not mail them. Instead, I tore them up and put them in the rubbish bin in the kitchen.

The following day, a Saturday, Enrique and I went shopping, as usual. We carried on with the routine that had been a part of our life for such a long time. I was very depressed and unhappy, but if he noticed, he did not say anything.

On Sunday, I went to church, again as usual. I could not handle the situation that I was in any longer because I was so deeply unhappy. I came home from church and told Enrique I wanted a separation. He seemed very agreeable to it and did not express any particular desire to stay with me.

On the Monday morning when I reported for work, I received a phone call within minutes of walking through the door. It was Enrique.

'You had an affair!' Enrique yelled at me over the telephone.

I was astonished. How did he know? I hadn't told a soul.

'I want you to come home right now!' Enrique demanded.

I was in a state of shock. I didn't know what to do. I went and told my supervisor that I had to go. I can only assume that he could see from the look on my face and the tone of my voice that it was serious.

I drove the 25 miles home in a state of terror. I knew Enrique was going to kill me when I got home, but I had no other choice but to face him. When I walked through the door, Enrique was holding Aaron. I wanted to take Aaron, but Enrique refused to let me have him.

Enrique's exact words to me were, 'I am going to take Aaron away from you and you will never see him again,' chillingly staring me in the eye. Enrique then took the letters that I had written and thrown away. When I asked him how he got the letters, he told me that he rummaged through the trash to find them. Enrique asked me how many times I slept with Patrick. I initially refused to tell him, but he hit me on the face with the full force of his fist several times until I relented and told him. The blows I sustained broke my nose and dislocated my jaw. As a result of his rage, I now have chronic sinusitis, which is a result of obstructed nasal airways, and I also have to wear a splint in my mouth every night to keep my jaw from dislocating.

Enrique then asked me why I slept with Patrick.

The only answer I could come up with was, 'Because he was nice to me.'

'Because he was nice to you?' Enrique sneered, 'Is that all it takes for you to sleep with someone?'

I did not know how to answer that question. I felt so ashamed. Enrique made me feel ashamed. Maybe if he had been nice to me in the first place I would not have felt the need to go outside of the marriage for a little love and affection.

Then, out of the blue, Enrique began hitting me with the full force of both of his fists. I cowered down to protect myself. He was hitting me on the head, back and neck, and I could feel myself losing consciousness. It was at that point that I knew he was going to kill me.

Before I lost consciousness I pushed Enrique back and fell on to the floor. I began crawling on my hands and knees and tried to make my way to the front door. I thought if I could get out of the house he would not kill me. Just before I reached the front door, Enrique jumped on top of me and pushed me to the floor. When he saw all of the blood on my uniform and my face, he started screaming, 'What have I done to you?' Then he yelled, 'We are getting a divorce! You are coming with me to the court house and I am divorcing you!'

Before I knew it, Enrique dragged me to the car, made me get in, and drove me to the local court house. I thought he was insane, but was in such a state of shock, said nothing about his manic behaviour. I just imagined him dragging me through the halls of the court house while yelling and screaming to anybody and everybody who would listen that he was divorcing me.

Somehow, a touch of reason entered Enrique's enraged mind and he decided he was not going to divorce me that day. He calmed down and we then drove back home.

As soon as I got home I told Enrique that I had to go back to work. Enrique asked me to stay home and spend the day with him, but that was something that I simply could not do. I therefore drove back to work with a black eye, broken nose and dislocated jaw, all given to me by my husband. I didn't even bother to change my shirt, which had my blood all over it. I must have looked a sight. Amazingly, my supervisor failed to send me to the hospital to have my injuries looked at, so I carried on working through the day.

That evening when I arrived home, I told Enrique that he had to leave. I could not live with him any more if he was going to beat me to the point of losing consciousness. It was at that point that I was fully conscious of the fact that my husband was capable of murder, and I was afraid that I would be his first victim.

Enrique then took it upon himself to ring his family and tell them what had happened. At their instigation, he asked me to stay with him for the sake of Aaron. Enrique did not want to stay with me from his own initiative, but only because his family wanted him to. That said it all about my husband.

I told Enrique that I did not want to stay with him, and cited two reasons. The first reason I gave for wanting to leave was because he had abandoned me to go on a Spanish holiday on my 23rd birthday when I was seven months pregnant. The second reason I gave was the fact that I did not get any support from him when Keith Holshouser and Herb Snedeker were harassing me. I had repressed the anger in me for such a long time and I simply could not forgive him any more for all of the things he had done, or failed to do, to harm me.

That night I slept in the spare bedroom, which is where I slept until Enrique left. I could not trust him not to harm me any more.

The following day we had to go to the travel office on Tyndall Air Force Base so Enrique could purchase a ticket to go back to Lawrence. We had lunch at the Burger King, but Enrique refused to eat his meal. All those years he had hurt me, mistreated me, and abused me just welled up inside of me. I could not contain my rage any more.

In retrospect, I feel very guilty about all the pain I caused him, and even wrote him a letter to apologise for my behaviour. My only excuse is that he had abused me so badly for so many years that he had pushed me to the point that I was becoming just as nasty as he was. I am not proud of the anger that I showed him, but I am only a human being capable of error and when I am put in an intolerable situation, I may not behave in the best fashion.

On the Thursday, which was the day that Enrique and Aaron left, he lost his ticket. I began yelling and screaming at him that he had better damn well find that ticket because he was leaving no matter what.

In the car on the way to the airport, I continued to yell and scream at Enrique. I told him what a lousy husband and lover he was. All of those years when I just accepted the humiliation and abuse welled up inside me. For the first time in years, I told Enrique how I felt. I could not control the anger that I felt towards my husband any longer.

When we were at the airport I kissed my son goodbye. I was not able to keep him with me because I did not have day-care sorted and was not allowed to take him to Germany with me.

I was so brainwashed by the military that it never even occurred to me that I could choose not to leave my son. I was so brainwashed by my husband that he made me believe that I was not a good mother.

When Enrique left, I tried to phone Patrick at the number he had given me for his work. The man who answered the phone asked me if I was his wife, which I found to be quite surprising. According to Patrick, he and his wife were separated. I can only guess that was just another lie he told me in an attempt to get me into his bed.

The next day I rang Patrick at his barracks on the Autovon network. When he realised it we me, he just said, 'Can I call you back?'

'Well, yes,' I replied, rather bemused at his response. Patrick put the phone down and I never heard from him again. It was at that point that I knew beyond a shadow of a doubt that I had been used. Patrick didn't give a damn about me or my feelings. Like the vast majority of men who walk the Earth today, he only cared about himself. He didn't lose even a moment's sleep over the part he played in the break-up of my marriage and family.

Although I was hurt about what Patrick did, I put him out of my mind. The only way my personality could survive was to forget all about it. I was so good at dissociating bad experiences that I even forgot his name.

A few days after Enrique and Aaron left my life, I went into the mental health clinic to speak to them about what had happened. I specifically told the person who spoke to me that I was feeling suicidal and was driving recklessly as a result. The individual spoke to me for about half an hour and then sent me on my way. There was no mention whatsoever about following up our meeting to make sure I was okay.

One concern I did express to the counsellor was the fact that I was afraid I would never be able to find anyone else to love. I was assured that, at only 24, I would have plenty of time to meet someone else. I was not so sure, however. As it turns out, my reservations were found to be quite prophetic. Although I would go on to have many loves in my life, the vast majority of them were entirely unsuitable for the development of my personality and soul.

The weekend after Enrique and Aaron left I had nothing to do, so went for a walk on the beach. I came across a young man who had rented a beach house with his group of friends for the weekend. It just so happened that he too was in the military and stationed at Tyndall Air Force Base. I agreed to meet up with the man the next day and he took me to his accommodation on base. I related to him the break-up of my marriage, and he must have seen how upset I was about the whole situation.

The young man responded to my anguish by trying to get me to go to bed with him. What I needed was a friend, but all he wanted was sex. Is that what men are all about? Are men intent upon satisfying their own sexual urges at all costs? Do men not care whom they hurt just so long as they are able to relieve the tension inside of themselves in the form of an ejaculation? If that is the only behaviour that men are capable of, no wonder the world we live in is such a depraved, unsafe place to be. If the only behaviour that men are capable of is despicable sex acts at the most inappropriate of times, I am very glad to be a woman!

The next time I went to the singles group, run by the mental health clinic, several people had commented to me that I had lost weight. The fact of the matter was that I had actually gained weight. I had just lost weight around the middle because I had been jogging every day.

From that point on, I would always have problems with my weight. I suppose I turned to comfort eating as a way to cope with the fact that my son had been taken from me. It is not an uncommon phenomenon. Many women, even those who had been abusive towards their children, have turned to overindulgence as a response to losing their children, either through death or an inability to care for them.

A girlfriend of a colleague invited me to stay with her for the two weeks remaining until I had to leave Cape San Blas, which was a highly thoughtful act of kindness. There are so many people in this terribly cruel world who will not do anything for anybody unless they think they can benefit personally from it, so her offer was a truly rare, selfless act.

This woman, however, was the sort of individual who was always on the go and needed to stay busy. She related to my colleague that all I ever wanted to do was sit around the house and watch television. What did she or anyone else expect from me? There wasn't much to do in Cape San Blas anyway, so unless one had a network of friends and family, one was pretty much at a loss for things to do

I had been through an awful ordeal and all I wanted was to be left alone. It is a shame, really, that nobody seemed to have any understanding at all for my depression and my past traumatic experiences. As always, most people are so wrapped up in themselves that they cannot see anything beyond their own personal wants, needs and desires.

I did try to go to the mall in Panama City, but that venture ended in disaster. I drove up there and parked my car in the huge parking lot. I walked into the mall all by myself, but was soon overwhelmed by the masses of people and all the shops. The emotional pain inside me was so great that it had transcended my psyche and I actually felt physical pain from my very deep depression. I was so awestruck by everyone bustling around me that I fled the mall in a state of high anxiety. That was the last time I tried to go out on my own in Florida.

I had never heard of agoraphobia, which is a fear of open spaces, and did not know that it is a classic symptom of post-traumatic stress disorder. But of course, nobody would ever see me as a victim. They would always view me as this horrible, evil woman who left my baby.

One day when I spoke to Enrique on the telephone, he asked me if I were pregnant. I could not understand why he would ask me such a thing. Surely he knew that I would not have allowed myself to become pregnant again. Once was enough. I immediately got a nauseous feeling in my stomach just thinking about getting pregnant. Falling pregnant was something that I never wanted to do again in a million years. The first experience was enough to put me off having children for the rest of my life.

Another thing I had to do was to pack and out-process all on my own. When the removal man came to pack my things, I naïvely sat in the living room and allowed him to work on his own. Because nobody was watching him, he took it upon himself to steal my wedding ring.

It was several months before I realised what the man had done. I did not begrudge him the ring because I did not want it any more. That wedding ring had brought me so much pain and heartache that I could not imagine how anyone wearing it could have any kind of happiness in this life. In fact, I felt sorry for the next person who would be wearing it.

Enrique had stopped wearing his wedding ring long ago. He 'lost' his first ring, so I bought him another one. He then promptly 'lost' that one as well. Quite obviously, for reasons that only Enrique will know, he did not want to wear a wedding ring. I declined to purchase another ring for him because I thought it was a waste of money if he were going to keep 'losing' it.

Enrique's behaviour towards me clearly indicated that he did not want to be married, and this ambivalence reflected in his refusal to wear a symbol of our marriage, such as a ring. I therefore cannot understand his attitude towards me: Enrique did not want me but he did not want anybody else to have me either.

I left Cape San Blas to go to Lawrence, Massachusetts, for two weeks before going to Germany.

I was totally numb inside. I was already beginning to dissociate the whole experience. Because I am an adult survivor of child abuse and neglect, and was forced to keep so many family secrets, it was second nature for me to forget what had happened. Forgetting, you see, was really the only way my personality could survive.

As in my childhood, my personality fragmented into a sub-personality that accepted the experience for me. Were it not for the many sub-personalities that graciously decided to accept all of the traumas and abuses for me, I would have either committed suicide or gone insane long ago.

The only recollection I have of many of my more difficult experiences is through flashbacks, when I remember just a small fragment of the more traumatic episodes. Even those fragmentary flashbacks, however, are enough to send me into a spiral of self-loathing and guilt.

My mind was generous enough to equip me with multiple personalities. Without multiple personalities, who have been gracious enough to step in during those times of intense stress, I would never, ever have made it through four decades of life.

For me, multiple personalities are not a mental illness or a personality disorder, but a way of living that has allowed me to survive a life of abuse and neglect that no person should ever have to endure.

Lawrence

When I stepped off the airplane in Boston's Logon airport, Enrique greeted me with a bouquet of flowers. I thought it was quite satirical that once our marriage was over, my husband had decided to buy me flowers. With the exception of our most recent anniversary, Enrique had never purchased me anything to show his appreciation for me. The one time

he should have bought me flowers, when I had just given birth to his son, none were forthcoming. Rather than being appreciative of what one would have thought was a generous gesture, I was bemused. The time for flowers, I felt, had long since passed.

Another thing I noticed about Enrique was that he had discarded his white Y-front underwear in favour of the European-style bikini underwear. I have to say that I did not like Enrique's new taste in underwear, as it appeared quite effeminate to me. I much preferred men to dress and behave like real men, and in my opinion real men did not wear bikini underwear; just as they didn't beat their wives.

When Aaron woke up the next morning, he was so pleased to see me that he crawled on my lap and went back to sleep for another two hours. When he woke up again, however, the bond had been broken. I can only suppose that he was afraid I would leave him again, and it is for that reason he rejected me from that point onward.

Aaron had been through a lot too. He had to witness my marital discord and his father brutally beating his mother, which deeply affected him. I did not know a name for it at the time, but

Aaron was suffering from an attachment disorder, which was brought about by the fact that I had to leave him because of the break-up of my marriage and my military duties.

I loved Aaron so much that I did not want to inflict any harm on him. In the years to follow, I could have very easily engaged in a nasty custody dispute, but who exactly would have benefited from such actions? It certainly would not have done Aaron any good. For the sake of Aaron's well-being, I left him where he was because I truly did not want to traumatise him any more than he had already been. It is such a shame, really, that his father did not take the same view and behave reasonably for the sake of his son.

I made the ultimate sacrifice so my son would have a chance at a better life than I had. Enrique, however, sacrificed nothing. His whole attitude was take, take, take; from me, from his parents, from the government, or from anybody else from whom he could garner sympathy. I had no idea at the time what a nasty leech my husband really was. He even kept Aaron because he knew he would get government benefit and would not be expected to work as a single parent. Enrique had no intention of going out and getting a job, which was why it was in his best interest to keep Aaron with him for as long as possible.

One thing that upset me was that Aaron had forgotten every single word I had taught him. I had always taken the time to talk to Aaron, teach him words, and make him laugh. Enrique, on the other hand did not do a thing with Aaron to assist him in his development. Enrique only saw Aaron as a meal ticket because he knew that as long as he had custody of Aaron he would be able to carry on milking money out of me and would not be expected to go out and get a job. It is for that reason that Enrique pretty much left Aaron to his own devices while he watched television, read books, or did pretty much anything else that he wanted to do while he was supposed to be caring for his son.

I noticed that whenever I gave Aaron a bath, he would push my hands away from him whenever I tried to clean his private parts.

He had never pushed me away from him before, and I was very concerned about his behaviour.

I had noticed that it was a habit of the men of that family to grab hold of the little boys' penises. The boys for the most part would try to get away from the men when they engaged themselves in such play. I personally did not think it was a very nice game for the men to play with the little boys in the family, but not being a member of that family, I thought it was a cultural difference and therefore said nothing about what was going on. Nobody else seemed to mind when the men would laugh and joke and grab hold of the penis of any young boy who was unlucky enough to be within arm's reach at the time.

In retrospect, whether what the men did was play or not, I do not feel that it was appropriate behaviour to be engaging in with a child. I will never know, however, if the men of that family decided to 'play' with my child in the same way that they played with other children. If they did, I think that their behaviour is tantamount to child abuse.

It is ironic, really, that I permitted my son to stay with his father and his paternal family because I felt they could give Aaron a much better life than I could give him. Looking back, I now realise that Enrique had too many problems with himself to ever give Aaron a good upbringing. If Enrique was not interested in providing for his wife then he would be equally uninterested in providing for his son.

When I was alone with Enrique's cousin, she confided to me something that was obviously a family secret. Ana, Enrique's aunt, told her daughter that she did not think our marriage would ever work out. Basically, she felt that Enrique was not the marrying kind and that he was a very hard person to live with. If she only knew the full extent of the demons that lurked within Enrique's psyche to make him an inappropriate husband and father!

Because it was hard to keep the family secret was that Enrique was not suitable for marriage, I have great difficulty in understanding how his family could conspire with him to deprive Aaron of a mother. If Enrique's entire family knows that he had too many personality problems to make any kind of a reasonable decision regarding women and marriage in general, then I simply do not understand their actions. Aaron's happiness and emotional welfare are what should have been of importance to those people, not getting even with me for any real or imagined transgression that I might have committed.

One morning I asked Enrique if he would get a job in Germany. I asked him to take a job in Germany because I wanted to be close to Aaron, but I did not reveal my true intentions to my husband.

'What are you trying to say?' Enrique asked me.

I could not answer that question. Enrique thought I wanted a reconciliation, but that was not what I wanted at all. All I wanted was to be near my son.

I have heard so many stories of women who left their children with their abusive husbands, only to return because they could not bear to be parted from their children. If Enrique had not been so violent towards me, I may very well have reconciled too. I was afraid, however, that if I did get back together with him, one day he actually would kill me.

To be honest, even twenty years after having lost my son to that man, after having exhausted every avenue to have contact with him, I might very well have put my life in jeopardy by reconciling with my violent, abusive husband. The problem lies in the fact that with the exception of extremely short, limited periods of time, I have never been without a male companion in my life, thereby complicating any reconciliations I may have attempted. One evening, in tears, I told my boyfriend of over four years that I wanted my son back so badly I was even thinking of going back to my husband. Needless to say, he was not very pleased, but made no comment. He had enough decency not to stand in the way of any such decision, should I decide to make it.

Lest it seem that I am being melodramatic to garner sympathy, the *Daily Express* published the following article on 23rd December 2002:

Women trying to end relationships are among those at most risk of being victims of domestic murder, police research revealed yesterday.

The study by the Metropolitan Police also showed that in 30 per cent of cases, pregnancy could be a trigger for violence from abusive partners.

Senior officers hope the research – which also found stalkers are more likely to be violent if they have had a relationship with their target – will help them intervene quicker in volatile situations to save lives.

The Met's Understanding and Responding to Hate Crime team examined all domestic murders and assaults in London over the past two years. They found around one in four murders in the capital are domestic. Notions of 'If I can't have her, then no-one can' are recurring features, said the report.

The work also found many incidents happen as a result of disputes over child custody.

After almost twenty years of being parted from Aaron, I was so desperate to have any contact at all with him that I actually contemplated telling Enrique that I was dying. If I had thought it would have achieved the desired result, of seeing Aaron, I would have done so. The sad part of this tale is that within a matter of weeks of my dreaming up the idea, I found out that my own father had been diagnosed with a very aggressive form of inoperable lung cancer. My own father was dying, and the knowledge of it saddened me greatly.

One evening Enrique and I went to a disco with his two sisters. Enrique's sisters were hoping we would resolve our differences and kept telling me what a good couple Enrique and I made. I did not feel like a good couple: I felt horrible.

That evening Enrique crawled into the bed in the corner of the room I had been sleeping in, his huge penis fully erect. It was quite clear to me exactly what he wanted, but just to make doubly sure I knew what his intentions were, my estranged husband told me he wanted to make love to me. I personally think he had to be a really sick and twisted individual to expect me to willingly be his lover after he had broken my nose and dislocated my jaw, but I suppose it takes all kinds to make a world.

I was absolutely amazed. I never considered what Enrique and I did to be making love. I always considered it to be just sex, and so did Enrique. It was only when we were on the verge of divorce that Enrique suggested we make love. I was totally repulsed at the thought of doing anything physical with him, and that especially included making love.

I told Enrique that I did not want to make love, and that was one of the few times I had asserted myself in our marriage. Enrique was never pleased when I said no, and he was especially displeased on that particular evening. He responded by becoming verbally abusive towards me, calling me names, and telling me that I was a 'cheap little piece of trash walking down the street'.

If I were such a cheap little piece of trash, I don't understand why he wanted to make love to me in the first place. I would have thought he would have been happy to see the back of me, my being so cheap and so forth. That, my friend, was not the case. It was Enrique who approached me in a sexual manner, not the other way around.

The following morning the disagreement escalated. I was at my wit's end and was sick and tired of Enrique's being really horrible to me. An argument ensued and for the first time, after years of abuse, I gave as good as I got. In my rage I took a glass of water and threw it all over Enrique.

I think Enrique was totally shocked. He was not accustomed to my fighting back. He had hurt me and hurt me and hurt me, and I had always taken whatever abuse he dished out, and for the first time I was simply not going to take it any more.

Enrique responded by phoning his 'counsellor' and making an appointment for the both of us to go see her. This woman was paid by CHAMPUS, a scheme that allowed Enrique to get free medical treatment off base, all courtesy of the United States Air Force. Enrique was not the victim that he tried to portray himself as. He was a very shrewd individual who knew every penny that he was entitled to, and made sure that he got it.

In retrospect I believe the woman who was 'counselling' Enrique was a very misguided individual who told him exactly what he wanted to hear so the money would keep rolling her way on a weekly basis.

The first thing the woman did was tell me that I was anorexic, even though I was actually a few pounds overweight. Enrique weighed in at about 120 pounds soaking wet, so if anybody was anorexic it was clearly he. Yet somehow, the 'counsellor' failed to notice that it was Enrique who was underweight and not I. Enrique had projected his own eating disorder onto me and his 'counsellor' acted as his accomplice.

The next thing that was brought up was the fact that I had had an affair. I did not consider it to be an affair, but more like a three-night stand. The 'affair' was something I preferred to forget. Even though Enrique made a song and dance about my being unfaithful to him, not one word was said about the way that he had treated me. As far as Enrique and his 'counsellor' were concerned, I was the guilty party in the demise of our marriage.

I doubt very seriously that Enrique had let his 'counsellor' know he had been physically and verbally abusive towards me. I am equally sure he failed to mention to his 'counsellor' that he had broken my nose, blackened my eye and dislocated my jaw. Enrique told the 'counsellor' exactly what he wanted her to believe and she in turn told him exactly what he wanted to hear.

Because counsellors often must rely on inaccurate information and only pander to the whims of their clients, I feel they quite often do more harm than good. It was certainly true in my case. Instead of Enrique's so called counsellor's focusing on my infidelity, she should have probed into why Enrique felt the need to quit his job, abuse his wife, and fail to provide for his family. If she had done that, however, Enrique would have run a mile. Enrique's 'counsellor' wanted his money too much to bring a few home truths to him. That woman knew very well if she did her job properly, she would not have any business, which is why she merely told her clients what they wanted to hear.

The very next thing that we discussed was the fact that I was Aaron's mother and I wanted him with me. The 'counsellor' then informed me that a court of law would not award me custody of Aaron because I could not provide a stable home for him. I left the meeting a defeated person. All I wanted was what was best for my son and that 'counsellor' told me his being with me was not good for him. Enrique was quite pleased with himself because his 'counsellor' had played his game by telling him exactly what he wanted to hear and telling me exactly what he wanted her to say.

After my two weeks in Lawrence, Massachusetts, were complete, I had to leave to go to Germany. I had to say goodbye to my son, whom I loved very much. The love I felt for Aaron could not compare with the love I felt for any other person. Having to leave him was one of the most difficult things I have ever had to do.

Saying goodbye to Aaron destroyed my soul.

Aftershock

I suppose things were never the same for me once I was forced to hand Aaron over to Enrique. I loved Aaron so much, and I only wanted what was best for him. It is such a shame, therefore, that his father did not feel the same way.

One story in the Bible will stay with me for the rest of my life. Kings I tells a tale about King Solomon, which I feel is reflective of my situation:

> Then there came two women that were harlots, unto the king and stood before him.
>
> 'And there was one woman said, O my lord, I and this woman dwell in one house; and I was delivered of a child with her in the house.
>
> And it came to pass the third day after that I was delivered, that this woman was delivered also: and we were together, there was no stranger with us in the house, save we two in the house.
>
> And she arose at midnight, and took my son from beside me, while thine handmaid slept and laid it on her bosom, and laid her dead child on my bosom.
>
> And when I arose in the morning to give my child suck, behold it was dead. But when I had considered it in the morning, it was not my son, which I did bear.
>
> And the other woman said, nay, but the living is my son, and the dead is thy son. Thus they spake before the king.
>
> They said to the king, the one saith, this is my son that liveth, and thy son is dead, and my son is the living.

And the king said, bring me a sword. And they brought a sword before the king.

And the king said, divide the living child in two, and give half to the one and half to the other.

Then spake the woman whose the living child was unto the king, for her bowels yearned upon her son, and she said, O my lord, give her the living child, and in no wise slay it. But the other said, let it be neither mine nor thine, but divide it.

Then the king answered and said, give her the living child, and in no wise slay it: she is the mother thereof.

Isn't it a shame that real life is not as fair as the Bible. In real life, the criminals walk free while the victims are given little, if any support. The fact is that Aaron was my child, not Enrique's. If Enrique had had his way, Aaron would not even be in this world. When I fell pregnant, Enrique asked me to have an abortion. The only reasons why Enrique wanted to keep Aaron was because he wanted to harm me, he knew that he could get all kinds of government benefit he would not otherwise have been entitled to, and he wanted an excuse not to have to go out and get a job by saying he had to take care of Aaron.

Many people believe I left because I did not want Aaron, but that is not true. I left because I had to leave to work and pay my and Aaron's way in this world.

I did not have a supporting family who were prepared to help me keep my son, and not one individual on the face of this Earth has ever told me they would help me get my son back. Now that is incredibly sad.

I simply did not have any fight left. I could not fight Enrique on my own and there was no one who was willing to confront my abusive husband on my behalf.

Enrique likes to pretend he is honourable, but honourable men don't sit back and do absolutely nothing while their wives work themselves to the point of physical and mental exhaustion. Honourable men don't beat their wives. And lastly, honourable men don't steal children from their mothers.

When I arrived in Neu Ulm, Germany, I received absolutely no support from anybody with regard to getting my son back. In fact, the opposite was true. The military did not want single parents among their ranks, so if I had Aaron with me, I would have had to give another person power of attorney to be his guardian. In addition, I had to go on deployment several times a year and would have had to arrange for someone to keep Aaron during that time.

When I rang Enrique and told him about my working situation, his reply was, 'I'm not letting Aaron go to Germany with you.'

Deep down in my heart I knew the military was not a suitable environment for a child, so I acquiesced.

Enrique also started a hate mail campaign. Whenever I wrote him a letter trying to be nice, he would respond with all of the venom and spite he could muster. So many times he reduced me to tears from the hateful things he said in his letters.

Even after we had separated, Enrique still caused me financial difficulties. He refused to cooperate, as usual, and would not fill out a joint tax return even though I had earned all of the money and had given him half of my reenlistment bonus. I therefore was found to owe the Internal Revenue Service a significant amount of money and it took me several years to get that debacle sorted out.

The following year when I moved to Prum Air Station, Germany, my misogynistic shop supervisor went to the section commander to do whatever he could to get me thrown out of the shop. I was therefore summoned into Captain Sasser, the section commander's office, and he proudly informed me he had read my medical records in their entirety. Even though he was not a health care professional and I had never given him permission to read my medical records, he felt that by virtue of his position in the military he was justified in doing so.

After Captain Sasser told me he had read my medical records, he informed me that he thought it was a good idea if I did not have my son with me because people who are abused usually go on to abuse others. Captain Sasser then went on to tell me that he was keeping his eye on me and I had better watch my step. I was particularly offended by what that man said because I had never been a discipline problem, yet he was insinuating I was. Thinking back, I find it incredulous that Captain Sasser should have spoken to me as he did, especially with regard to my son.

The fact is that my son was staying with the man who abused me, so it is not unreasonable to assume that if Enrique would abuse me then he would likely go on to abuse Aaron when he matured and developed his own personality. I do not understand, therefore, why Captain Sasser felt it was perfectly acceptable for my son to stay with his highly volatile father and not acceptable to say with his mother, who had never harmed another living soul in her life and who had only ever acted in self-defence.

The fact is that men (and women) who abuse women (and men) quite often go on to abuse children. Thus it is inappropriate for a child to stay with a man who has abused women because it is highly likely that he will go on to abuse the children in his care. But of course I did not know all of that when I handed Aaron over to my wife-beating husband. If I had known that men who abuse women usually abuse children as well, I would never have allowed my son to stay in his care. I can only assume, therefore, that Captain Sasser was either not in possession of all of the facts or was a highly misguided individual.

I had a boyfriend, Whit, who had at one time been a photographer for the Office of Special Investigations. He told me of some of the very unusual sights he had been required to photograph. Because of all that Whit had seen, he expressed to me grave concerns about Aaron's welfare. Whit told me that as soon as Aaron grew up and started to develop a personality in his own right, Enrique would attempt to control him in the same manner that he tried to dominate me.

I was in such a state of denial about the whole situation with Aaron that I simply could not understand what Whit was trying to tell me. I believed Enrique loved Aaron and would never harm him. But then again, I had always believed Enrique would never harm me either, and look what he did.

If Enrique truly loved Aaron, he would put aside his personal feelings for me and would have tried to get along with me for Aaron's sake. Enrique would have done what was best for Aaron. No decent man deprives his child of a mother. The fact is that Enrique never loved Aaron. Aaron was just another person whom Enrique could exercise control over.

An unknown author has written an article and placed it on the internet, entitled, 'Separation – A Half Life: More Than Grief – Not Quite Death'. I found the piece to be quite reflective of my situation and have therefore included it in this work:

A number of mothers have mentioned the guilt they have felt in not having grieved the loss of their baby at the time of surrender – how they felt a total numbness for years and often decades afterward. As a result, it was decided to include a personal, non-identifying psychiatric diagnosis in the hope of helping others understand why this might have occurred, by explaining how a sound mind protects itself from unbearable distress by shutting off from the trauma until a trigger event occurs where the mind is no longer able to repress the event.

For too long, adoption separation has been minimised by being referred to at best as grief and loss, at worst something we are often expected to 'get over' and put behind us. Some of us even thought we had – but had we really?

The possible reason many mothers have been unable to

speak of their experience is because their experience had become unspeakable, i.e., to speak of it is to make it real – and to make it real is to then have to face their loss – something many were unable to do until adoption legislation gave them hope, bringing their as-if-dead babies to life and making them real again.

Naturally the length of and depth of dissociation differs from mother to mother depending on 'trigger' events bringing her out of denial, i.e., some mothers do not block out the experience but cannot access their grief until much later; some grieved immediately and then blocked out the whole, racking experience for years.

Some mothers blocked out entirely for years or decades, their grief manifesting itself in other forms – at other objects or life events. Some remain dissociated even when they have met their adult child and cannot access reality until some years after reunion (this often results in delayed emotional bonding between mother and child, at least for a time).

For some mothers, the pain of their experience and brainwashing is so deep they may never allow themselves to access their own reality and sometimes place vetoes or deny their relationship with their searching child, disclaiming (as was required of them) that their maternal instincts even existed; some spend their lives denying the existence of their child and cannot physically or psychologically fall pregnant again or until a trigger event (e.g., entitlement) forces them to be no longer able to deny.

For many, the combination of sedation, trauma, not seeing the baby and so forth, causes the mind to manifest an unreal quality regarding their experience, the picture never becoming quite clear until or unless some tangible information is acquired to help piece it all together, e.g., obtaining medical records, social work reports, revisiting the unwed mothers' home/hospital, speaking to other mothers with the same experience and with whom they can identify, et cetera.

For some, the moment of dissociation is upon signing consent, when their unborn was taken at the moment of birth, when the revocation period had expired, when they attempted to reclaim their baby only to be told it was too late.

For others, that moment of dissociation occurred much earlier – some time after their pregnancy was diagnosed, when they were told the foetus they were carrying was not their baby but already belonged to someone else, that they could not keep their baby. When it became obvious that their condition was seen by others as a problem to be gotten rid of, when all hope was gone and no-one had saved them at the eleventh hour after all; or when they were forbidden to see their child and did not know how to ask, or when they asked and were ignored.

Sometimes it is impossible to dissociate and mothers turned to a lifetime of drugs, alcohol, anti-depressants, et cetera, to get themselves through. Tragically, some took the permanent way out.

Those mothers who do survive the loss of a child often suffer from a severe psychiatric syndrome. There are features of distinct personality modes, but not of the pattern described under multiple personality disorder. There are features of psychogenic amnesia and also major features of depersonalisation. When the protective aspects of their separation have been threatened, such as being forced to acknowledge that the baby was surrendered, major depression can occur. Dissociative disorder is mostly precipitated by acute shock, loss or trauma. The psychopathology is an attempted adaptation to unbearable pain and distress. The nature of this mental state would totally preclude the mother from making any claim, yet it is entirely caused by the matter about which a mother would make a claim.

The End